ITALIAN PRIDE

ITALIAN PRIDE
101 Reasons to Be Proud You're Italian

FEDERICO AND STEPHEN MORAMARCO

Illustrations by Patricia Peacock-Evans

CITADEL PRESS
Kensington Publishing Corp.
www.kensingtonbooks.com

Dedicated to the memory of Stephen Moramarco
and Nina Toriello Moramarco,
who left us the heritage described in these pages

CITADEL PRESS books are published by

Kensington Publishing Corp.
850 Third Avenue
New York, NY 10022

All Kensington titles, imprints, and distributed lines are available at special quantity discounts for bulk purchases for sales promotions, premiums, fund raising, educational, or institutional use. Special book excerpts or customized printings can also be created to fit specific needs. For details, write or phone the office of the Kensington special sales manager: Kensington Publishing Corp., 850 Third Avenue, New York, NY 10022, attn: Special Sales Department, phone 1-800-221-2647.

Kensington and the K logo Reg. U.S. Pat. & TM Office
Citadel Press is a trademark of Kensington Publishing Corp.

First printing October 2000

10 9

Printed in the United States of America

Library of Congress Cataloging-in-Publication Data

Moramarco, Federico.
    Italian pride : 101 reasons to be proud you're Italian / Federico and Stephen Moramarco.
        p.   cm.
    ISBN 1-55972-512-5 (hc)
    1. Italy—Civilization.   2. National characteristics, Italian.
    3. Italians—United States—Ethnic identity.   4. Cookery, Italian.
    I. Moramarco, Stephen.   II. Title
    DG442.M67   1999
    945—dc21   99-12773
                                                                           CIP

Contents

Acknowledgments

The following titles were particularly useful:

Anderson, Burton. *Treasures of the Italian Table* (New York: William Morrow, 1994).

Barzini, Luigi. *The Italians* (New York: Bantam 1965).

Mangione, Jerre, and Ben Morreale. *La Storia: Five Centuries of the Italian American Experience* (New York: Harper Collins, 1992).

Mariani, John. *The Dictionary of Italian Food and Drink* (New York: Broadway Books, 1998).

Root, Waverly. *The Food of Italy* (New York: Vintage Books, 1971).

We also found the many Italian American websites very helpful. Particular note should be made of the Italian-American website of New York: http://www.italian-american.com/main.htm.

Special thanks is due to Patricia Peacock-Evans for her wonderful illustrations; Carrie Cantor for her many ideas that enlivened the book and for her keen editorial eye that sharpened its prose; and our agent, Julie Castiglia, for her support. And we owe a special debt of gratitude to Nico Calavita and Gennaro Santangelo, who made many valuable suggestions.

Introduction

In Italy nothing is more important than *la famiglia* (the family); the foundation of all things Italian can be traced to that venerable institution. The pride of being Italian is something that is passed on from parent to child, and so we write this book as father and son, intending to convey what is best and most notable in our heritage. Italian pride is neither a boast nor an attempt to create a sense of superiority. Rather, it is a feeling of well-being and a connection to a long tradition of passion, excellence, and accomplishment. It nurtures our identity and supports our sense of self-esteem in an increasingly fragmented world. As each generation of Americans moves further away from its immigrant origins, it becomes more and more urgent to recognize the talents and gifts that we have contributed to our adopted country by way of our heritage.

We have divided the book into four sections: culture and history; places; people; and food. Italian culture and history, the foundations of Italian pride, have a rich legacy, embracing everything from hand gestures to the Mona Lisa, from opera to the expressive beauty of the Italian language. Italian places are distinctive geographic entities; cities like

Naples, Rome, and Venice and locales like the Italian Riviera, the Isle of Capri, and even the many "Little Italys" in America are unforgettable once experienced. People of Italian background who have made major contributions to a wide range of fields constitute the third section of the book. A mere listing of a few names—Leonardo da Vinci, Michelangelo, Supreme Court Justice Antonin Scalia, Frank Sinatra, and Madonna—suggests something of both the historical and current influence of Italians on our contemporary world. Finally, we come to food, which is central to the Italian character. Italian restaurants are ubiquitous throughout the world; pasta and pizza can be ordered in Bangkok, Beijing, and Boston. A brief overview of some of the characteristic elements of Italian food (including some recipes) are described to encourage you to try your hand at re-creating the Italian culinary experience at home.

We believe that it is essential for individuals with an Italian background to recognize the contributions of their ancestors and to pass on a sense of Italian pride to their children and grandchildren. We hope this book—a combination tour guide, cookbook, historical and biographical synopsis, and philosophical primer on all things Italian—will help you to do just that.

PART I

CULTURE AND HISTORY

1

Amore

The very word runs off the tongue like a poem: *amore,* a word that stirs the Italian soul and conjures up visions of life's possibilities. Socrates said that "the unexamined life is not worth living," but for Italians it is a life without love that is the life not worth living. Without amore, life is a thin gruel of getting and spending, a succession of repetitive days and nights without purpose or point. But with it—Ah, with it—the stars take on a shimmering gleam, the days pulse with sunlight and hope, the lovers transcend the workaday world, immersed in the magic of communion and the marriage of two souls.

Why is this passion for love and life so Italian? The Mediterranean climate? The elaborate courtship rituals that have developed between young men and women in the small hill towns of the country? The veneration of women that seems imprinted on the Italian male soul? The intense verbal passion that is the essence of Italian family life? Whatever the reason, there is no question that Italy is a synonym for romance and that the very air of the country resonates with the music of love. Mention Venice and what comes to mind but a gondolier serenading two lovers under the moonlight? Honeymooners flock to the Isle of Capri like pilgrims seeking a miracle, and surely there are more bridal shops in Naples than in any other city in the world.

For Italians, amore sustains life itself. There is no such thing as a halfhearted love. One succumbs completely to Cupid's lure, and life without the loved one present results in unbearable loneliness. The great Italian tenor from Tuscany Andrea Bocelli, whose wonderfully romantic voice seems the quintessence of amore, sings of this all-inclusive passion.

In music, art, poetry, and mythology and folktales, Italians have always been in love with love. The Greeks called her Aphrodite, but the Romans gave us Venus, the goddess of love, whom we can visualize as the Renaissance artist Botticelli painted her, emerging from a seashell in all of her naked splendor, the epitome of feminine beauty. The painting, *Birth of Venus*, which hangs in the Uffizi Gallery in Florence, takes your breath away as you pass it because you know that in Italy you, too, will fall under the goddess's spell.

2

Automobiles

Italians have contributed a unique combination of elegance, beauty, style, and speed to the sports car. Their sleek, provocative designs have seduced the world. The cars rank high among collectors as priceless treasures, and gleeful owners pamper the machines as if they were fine racehorses. The names of some of the most famous, Alfa-Romeo, Lamborghini, Maserati, and Ferrari, conjure up images in our heads of swift, speeding fantasy vehicles that will whisk us away to the world of our dreams.

The Italian romance with the automobile began with the turn of the twentieth century. Although the automobile was invented elsewhere, it was Italians who endowed it with their special brand of passion. From the earliest machines made in Italy it was clear that these cars were more than just shiny pieces of metal; they had a heart and soul.

One of the first Italian cars, and still one of the most treasured, is the Alfa-Romeo. Nicola Romeo, the company's founder, had no idea he would become one of the grandfathers of the sports car; his company began by producing mining machinery and agricultural equipment. After World War I ended in 1918, he surrounded himself with the finest designers and engineers and began producing engines for all kinds of machines, including the automobile. He continually produced slick new models and robust engines for the growing racing division that consistently left the Germans and English in the dust.

Then a young man named Enzo Ferrari joined the Alfa-Romeo team in 1920, initially as a driver. Here is where sports-car history shifts into second. By the time Ferrari left the company in 1929, Alfa-Romeo was the leader of the pack. With the knowledge gained from working at Alfa, Ferrari went on to start his own line of cars, which have become the benchmark for all automobiles of superior quality.

Bugatti and Lancia are other magical names of Italian wonder vehicles, and even Fiat has had its master machines. On the outside, under the hood, and in the driver's seat, Italian car designers have done much to raise the emotional level of even the most mundane commute.

To own one of these machines is the epitome of "having it all." They are not only automobiles but also works of art, interactive sculptures. They are scribbles in da Vinci's notebooks come gloriously to life in cherry red, with Michelangelo's intense passion harnessed under the hood. The car is the brush, the road the canvas, the drive the creation.

3

Cinema

The passionate and vivacious personalities of Italians have always made them stellar attractions on the screen.

First of all, there's *Ladri di Biciclette* (*The Bicycle Thief*, 1948), directed by the incomparable Vittorio De Sica. The story of a man and his search for his stolen bicycle marks the beginning of neorealism in film, in which the lives of real men and women are portrayed in simple, natural settings. The desperation of the lead character, Antonio, who must find the bicycle in order to keep his job, is a moving illustration of impoverished postwar Italy. This classic film won a special Academy Award in 1950 (before there was a category for foreign films).

Roberto Rossellini, another important director from the neorealist era, portrayed Italian society as it really was, often using real people instead of actors. His film *Open City* (1946) chronicles the Italian underground resistance during World War II.

In the sixties, Sergio Leone, with his action-packed *Fistful of Dollars*

(1964), starring Clint Eastwood, gave a new edge to the Western and a new star to the world. Leone's flair for dramatic situations, coupled with Ennio Morricone's unforgettable soundtrack, have often been imitated but never surpassed. The "spaghetti Western," as the style is lovingly known, is an art form all its own.

Another landmark director during this period is Michelangelo Antonioni, whose film *Blowup* (1966) is a surreal, ultramodern murder mystery that is a feast for the eyes and a challenge to the mind.

Following the tradition of commedia dell'arte, Italians know how to make hilarious comic films as well. *Pane e Ciocolata* (*Bread and Chocolate*, 1973), starring Nino Manfredi and Anna Karina, is one shining example of classic Italian comedy, which is about a young Italian man desperately trying to find work in Switzerland. The film has many memorable moments—including Manfredi's job at a chicken farm where the farmers live and act like birds—that are truly hilarious.

In the romance department, the locales alone are almost enough to get the emotions flowing. Franco Zeffirelli's *Romeo and Juliet* (1968) is one of the greatest adaptations of Shakespeare's play to be captured on film. Through lush images and passionate performances, Zeffirelli redefined cinema romance. *Il Postino* (*The Postman*, 1994), written by and starring beloved Neapolitan comedian Massimo Troisi, is about a Sicilian postman who learns about life, love, and poetry from exiled poet Pablo Neruda. Troisi, who worked hard for many years to bring this script to the screen, died the day after filming was completed. The movie became an instant classic.

The popularity of Italian cinema continues to grow as more and more great films and artists emerge from the region. Recently, the multitalented actor-writer-director Roberto Benigni won international recognition for his powerful film *La Vita È Bella,* (*Life Is Beautiful,* 1997). Benigni has long been popular in Italy, christened by admirers as "the Italian Charlie Chaplin" for his rare combination of humor and pathos. *La Vita È Bella,* the story of a heroic Italian-Jewish father who tries to protect his son from the horrors of the Holocaust, blends comedy and drama in such an original way that critics and viewers around the world joined together in praise. Benigni's jubilant behavior—clambering across the seats—at the Academy Awards when he won the award for Best Actor, is now part of Oscar history.

This is only a starting point for the variety of Italian movies that make them among the very best in the world. Grab a tub of good old American popcorn and enjoy!

4

Commedia dell'Arte

Italians can be proud of giving the world many good, hearty laughs. Comedy became a rich medium of expression with the development of Commedia dell'Arte. Throughout the streets of Europe, traveling Italian commedia troops would set up their makeshift playing area, wear outrageous masks, do acrobatics, and create wildly hilarious episodes in the life of the *Zanni*, the lovable stock characters of the trade.

First, there was Arlecchino, or Harlequin, a symbol of folly that has become famous around the world. He was crafty and smooth, wearing a black half mask and patchwork clothing, and caused general mayhem. His partner in crime was known as Colombina, a sexy and vivacious servant who wore similar dress and assisted and/or foiled her man's adventures.

Then there was Pulcinella, a master of disguise who dressed in white, wore a hat and a phallic nose, and lusted after the ladies. And the

Dottore, the doctor, who spoke in bizarre dialects and bungled all attempts to cure patients. Throw in Pantalone, a gullible merchant and Capitan, a braggart who was really a coward, and you have the makings of a caper filled with wild possibilities.

All of the plays were improvised; the actors relied solely on their quick wit, agile feet, and audience recognition of their character to guide them through the act. From these improvisations, troupes would develop comic bits, or *lazzi,* that could be repeated whenever needed to spice up the action. As the popularity of commedia dell'arte grew, actors developed hundreds of additional characters, each with a distinctive name and behavior that were instantly recognized by the crowds.

The events onstage were outrageous, and no one was spared a ribbing. The heroes were always the servants, like Arlecchino and Colombina, outwitting the bourgeois upper-class twits. Since the comedy was primarily physical, it crossed all language barriers as well. Because the actors wore masks, there was a greater amount of freedom as to what they could say or do. One of the most famous of the early troupes, the Golosi, were so bawdy that they caused commedia to be banned in France for thirty years!

Still, commedia reigned supreme in the world of the theater for two hundred years, and its influence extends to the present day. The French eventually adopted Harlequin to their own devices, and the medium's improvisational acting skills have influenced everything from vaudeville to *Saturday Night Live* and a wide range of TV sitcoms. Some of Shakespeare's plays, such as *As You Like It* and *The Comedy of Errors*, were undoubtedly drawn from commedia, as was his lovable buffoon Falstaff. The Marx Brothers, the Three Stooges, Bugs Bunny, and Mel Brooks owe many of their characterizations to the Italian art form.

The next time you see a movie or play or watch a television show that makes you laugh out loud, see if you can spot Pantalone, Arlecchino, or the Dottore nestled in the framework of the script. The Italian influence is surely there, poking you in the ribs and tickling your funny bone.

5

Convivio

There is no exact English-language translation for the Italian word *convivio*. "Conviviality" might be a cognate, but that word just doesn't quite do it. Convivio is a distinctly Italian kind of hospitality centered around the enjoyment of good food, good wine, family, and friends. A familiar scene in so many films with Italian subject matter will show a large group of people sitting around a long table, talking and gesturing passionately as they pass dishes to one another, pour wine, and break bread.

In our family, Grandfather Moramarco always began holiday meals by spilling a few drops of wine on the pristine white-linen tablecloth as he said, "*Buon' apetitito.*" He did this to make guests feel at home and not worry about making a mess. Naturally, Grandmother Moramarco was none too thrilled with the tradition, but that gesture is the essence of convivio.

When people are entertained in your home, the most important thing is that they feel relaxed and enjoy themselves. Convivio has nothing to do with elegant tablecloths, fine china, sterling silverware, crystal glasses, and the like. It has everything to do with taking pleasure in good conversation, enjoying a long, lingering, wonderful meal, and being surrounded by people you love and care for. It is the very antithesis of "fast food," a sad American innovation that unfortunately has slowly made some inroads in Italy, although the resistance to it there remains strong.

The word is derived from the Latin verb *convivere,* which means to live together, but the Italian sense of it means specifically to eat together and to do it with great enjoyment and pleasure. Italians generally make wonderful hosts—one of the reasons, perhaps, that so many of them have thrived in the restaurant business, where convivio is essential to success. People don't return to restaurants in which they don't feel comfortable.

But convivio has less to do with restaurants than it does with carrying on a tradition of hospitality at home. If you want to experience it, invite the people you love best over to dinner one night and spend the time with them enjoying their company, the abundant food you have prepared for the occasion, some fine Italian wine, and all the laughter, good talk, warmth, and love that the evening generates. You'll want to do it again and again. And tell your friends to watch out—because convivio is contagious.

6

Folktales

There is nothing more enchanting than a story from the old country. As do those from many other cultures, Italians have passed down the art of spinning a tale for generations, resulting in a legacy of stories reaching far back into the history of the land. While themes and plots are often universal, the Italian folktale has its own unique style and magic.

Such stories evolved before the era of the Internet, television, radio, and even the printing press. Sitting around the table or relaxing in the fields after a hard day's work, Italians found that hearing a spoken tale was an exciting way to pass the time. It wasn't until the latter part of the nineteenth century that people throughout Italy began to collect the *novelline* of their culture in print. In Sicily, Guiseppe Pietrè's *Fiabe, Novelle e Racconti Popolari Siciliani* (*Sicilian Fables, Stories, and Popular Tales*) was one of the most extensive of these collections, with some three hundred narratives written in Sicilian dialect. Other regions had their scholars, including Carolina

Coronedi-Berti in Bologna and Domenico Giuseppi Beroni, who recorded dozens of Venetian tales.

What emerges when one looks at these tales is an unmistakable style and beauty that are distinctly Italian. More often than not, the narrator is an important character; that role is usually given to a woman. In Pietrè's collection, the narrator is Agatuzza Messia, an old quiltmaker who, although illiterate, has a flair for the language of the people. When reading passages from her stories, you not only get a sense of the story but also a feeling of the manner in which these tales were originally passed on.

Unlike folklore in other countries, Italian folktales are rarely overtly violent and nearly all end harmoniously. Of course, love is a predominant theme. Whether it's a pig that turns into a king or a half-man who becomes whole, there is almost always an amorous uniting of man and woman. In the *fiaba,* or fairy tale, a mystical kingdom is invariably woven from words that excite the imagination.

The celebrated Italian novelist Italo Calvino has done a wonderful job of collecting, interpreting, and embellishing some of the best in his *Italian Folktales,* a must-have volume for anyone with an imagination. This definitive collection takes Italy's favorite legends and the art of Italian storytelling to the level of—and beyond—the Brothers Grimm.

One of our favorite tales, which was adapted and abridged from Calvino's collection, is about a very smart young woman and a very lucky king. It's called "Catherine, Sly Country Lass."

There was a farmer who had a very intelligent daughter. When he found a solid gold mortar and wanted to present it to the king, Catherine knew the king would wonder where the pestle was: she was right. The king was impressed by Catherine's smarts, and ordered her to make shirts for a regiment of soldiers from a tiny bit of wool. Catherine, in return, sent a handful of tiny threads back to king, saying he must first make a loom from these before she could make the shirts. Back and forth went the interaction between the king and Catherine, each trying to top the other with their witty requests. When he told her to appear neither clothed nor naked, on a stomach neither full nor empty, not in the day or night, and neither on horseback or on foot, she appeared wearing a fishnet after eating an apple at daybreak, riding a goat. Finally, there was nothing to do but get married. On their wedding night, the king told Catherine she must never meddle in his court business, knowing that she was smarter than he was. Of course, she couldn't resist, and the king became very angry. He told her that she could take the thing she liked best of all from the palace, and with that return home to her father the next morning. That night at dinner, she made sure the king overindulged and passed out. While he was sleeping, she took the king and his throne to her father's house in the country. When he awoke the next morning, the king wondered what was going on. "You told me to take the thing I liked best of all and take it home, so I took you." The two lovers laughed, made up, and the king appeared with his wife in the court from that day on.

Now there's a story of which both Italian men and women can be proud!

7

The Godfather Trilogy

Director Francis Ford Coppola's riveting adaptation of Mario Puzo's novel *The Godfather* tells the epic tale of an Italian family's rise to power in the ugly world of organized crime. To dismiss these films as "gangster movies" or to say that their depiction of the Mafia stereotypes Italians is to sell this masterpiece short, for it is a rich, human family drama.

What makes these films so special are the portrayals of characters by some of the finest actors in American film. Marlon Brando, although not Italian American himself, is one of the most highly respected actors of the twentieth century. He plays Don Corleone, the leader of the Corleone family. Brando's Corleone is a wise, tough man whose rise to power is due to the *rispetto* (respect) he receives from the people who surround him. As the century surges forward, Corleone's old-fashioned ways appear outmoded as the trafficking of narcotics begins to tear the families apart. A devastated Corleone watches as most of his sons and associates are brutally murdered. The only hope is that his son Michael (brilliantly played by Al Pacino) will use the gifts of his intelligence to make the family legitimate. In an emotional high point of the film, he laments Michael's growing involvement in a life of crime: "I never wanted this for you. I work my whole life—I don't apologize—to take care of my family, and I refused to be a fool dancing on the string held by all those big shots." Don Corleone's motivation, as twisted as the underworld he operates has become, is not greed or hunger for power but concern for the welfare of his family. By the first film's end, Don Corleone's hopes for his son's liberation from a life of crime and violence are shattered as Michael takes over the family business.

Brando received an Academy Award for his performance, and the film itself won for Best Picture that year. Coppola elevated Mario Puzo's compelling novel to Shakespearean heights. The kings and houses have been replaced by Mafia dons and their families, but the tragedy is just as strong. Corleone, like King Lear, wastes away as his family feuds. Each chapter of the trilogy deepens our understanding of the characters and the world in which they live.

In *The Godfather Part II* (1974), Michael's rise to power in the 1960s is contrasted with the story of a young Don Corleone's (Robert De Niro) immigration to America and subsequent induction into a life of crime. In what has been called the best film sequel of all time, *Part II* examines the characters of these two generations, giving us a chance to see what really makes them tick. The film's portrayal of Italian immigrants' hardships in America is especially captivating. It, too, won the Oscar for Best Picture and was the first sequel in history to actually receive more awards than the original.

The Godfather Part III (1990) is the final chapter in the trilogy. While not as powerful as the first two films, it does have some inspiring moments and performances and brings dignified closure to the Corleone saga.

The Godfather trilogy has inspired countless other films and filmmakers and assured each of its stars a place in cinema history. Coppola is considered one of our greatest directors. Nino Rota's unforgettable "Speak Softly Love" theme evokes powerful emotion. Pacino, De Niro, and many of the film's other actors and actresses have established themselves as major stars. The list of accolades goes on and on.

But when one looks to *The Godfather* for Italian pride, it is important not to get lost in the violence and the crime that pervades the films. While there can be no doubt that the criminal actions in the film represent the callous disregard for human life demonstrated by the Mafia, ultimately the films are about love, respect, honor, and family— a combination of virtues that are at the very core of Italian life.

8

Hand Gestures

Communicating in Italian involves more than uttering words and forming sentences. The words and sentences have nuances that must often be given shape in space. An Italian whose hands are tied is, in some ways, rendered speechless.

Walking down the streets of Italy, particularly in the south, you will see animated Italians hopping up and down, gesticulating wildly. A cupped hand shaking at the wrist. Two palms pressed together, pivoting in unison. A hand flicked under the chin. They're not just talking; they're giving life to the words that go beyond speech. "*Che cosa?*" "*Madonna!*" "*Basta!*" "*Tu si pazzo!*" Even if you don't speak a word of Italian, if you see the accompanying gesture, you get a sense of what is being conveyed.

Ask an Italian for directions and suddenly he or she is one with you, the terrain, and your ultimate destination. They may be saying "*Sinestra a la chiesa* (left at the church), *sulla collina* (up the hill), *e sempre diritto!* (and straight ahead)," but the words really don't matter much; their hands become churches, streets, stoplights, rivers, monuments.

The Italians have turned communication of this kind into an art form. A dance of the spirit. It is the joyous physical manifestation of emotion and conviction that can't be trapped in the uttered phrase. There is a physicality to the Italian culture that makes these gestures a natural extension of the language. When two Italians meet, a mere handshake will not suffice. Male or female, young or old, the two parties must embrace and give the other a friendly kiss on each cheek. It is this exchange that forms the basis of the communication that follows: friendly, intimate, and animated.

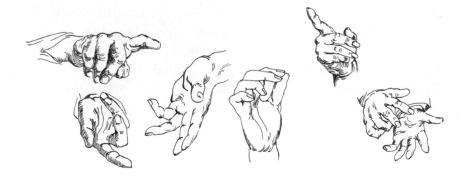

9

Hollywood Hot Shots

From the earliest days of the motion-picture industry, Italians have played a vital role in all aspects of filmmaking. One of the first films to deal with Italians was called, appropriately enough, *The Italian* (1915). This silent film told the story of a young man's immigration to America and the injustices he faced there.

A few years later, one of the first sex symbols of Hollywood appeared, an Italian by the name of Rudolph Valentino. *The Four Horsemen of the Apocalypse* (1921) launched a career that had audiences swooning. Many films followed, but he is perhaps best remembered for his role as Ahmed in *The Sheik* (1921). With his face partially hidden behind a veil, Valentino's large, round eyes won the hearts of many a filmgoer. When he died in New York in 1926, eighty thousand mourners showed up, causing a near riot. Mayhem also ensued at a *second* funeral on the West Coast.

More than seventy years later, people are still falling in love with

Italians. Leonardo DiCaprio is the latest in a long list of Italian heart-throbs to grace the silver screen.

But it's not just their good looks that have brought them success in the movie business, for many great Italians have toiled behind the scenes as well. For decades Frank Capra enjoyed the status of one of Hollywood's most popular directors. Aside from directing such classics as *It Happened One Night* (1934) and *Mr. Smith Goes to Washington* (1939), Capra will always be remembered for *It's a Wonderful Life* (1946). Starring James Stewart, this feel-good Christmas story has found a worldwide audience that continues to grow year after year.

By contrast, one of Hollywood's hottest directors today is Quentin Tarantino, who, because of his gritty crime dramas *Reservoir Dogs* (1992), *Pulp Fiction* (1994), and *Jackie Brown* (1997), could be considered the *anti*-Capra. His directoral style is tough and unrelenting, much like that of his heroes Martin Scorsese and Francis Ford Coppola.

Many great films offer a glimpse into the daily lives of Italian Americans in a frank, human, and sometimes humorous manner, exposing the rich Italian heritage to a mainstream audience. *Moonstruck* (1987), starring Nicolas Cage (a real Italian, in spite of his surname) and Cher is a lighthearted look at opposites attracting. Cher plays Lorretta Castorini, a widow who falls in love with Ronny Cammareri (played by Cage), the brother of the man she is supposed to marry. Set against the backdrop of a moonlit New York City, this is a wonderful, touching comedy. More recently, actor-writer-director Stanley Tucci's *Big Night* (1996) portrayed two Italian brothers struggling to make it in the restaurant business as they prepare the meal of their lives for the great Louis Prima, rumored to be coming to their restaurant for dinner. Few films have displayed the attitude of Italians toward food better than this one, and it's hard to watch it on an empty stomach!

Italian-American actors are always on Hollywood's A-list: Robert De Niro and Al Pacino, stars of *The Godfather* trilogy (see chapter 7) and other landmark films of the twentieth century have set the standard for serious actors of their generation. Marisa Tomei, star of *My Cousin Vinny* (1992), won an Academy Award for Best Supporting Actress for her comic role. Four years later Mira Sorvino, daughter of acclaimed actor Paul Sorvino, won the same award for her comic breakthrough performance in Woody Allen's *Mighty Aphrodite* (1995). Anne Bancroft and Susan Sarandon, also of Italian-American descent, have been honored with Academy Awards as well.

In front of and behind the camera, inside and outside the studio, in megablockbusters and in small, independent films, Italians have made their mark on American film history. Intense, emotional, volatile, and romantic, they have brightened the hours we spend in darkness staring at the silver screen.

10

Immigrants

Although it can accurately be said that Italians were the first Europeans to emigrate to America—think of Christopher Columbus and Amerigo Vespucci—the first major wave of emigration from Italy to America occurred in the late 1870s, coinciding with the time Italy declared itself a unified nation. That unity, however, came at a great price. Living conditions in the area south of Rome known as the Mezzogiorno (where 80 percent of the immigrants came from) were deplorable. The earliest immigrants came to America not so much to get rich but merely to survive.

However, it did not take long for "La Merica," as the early immigrants called it, to become known as a Promised Land in which money was easy to be had, where one was free to start over and make a new, prosperous life. The new arrivals, lonely for family and friends back home, wrote exaggerated accounts of the "good life" that lured more and more Italians to the ports of Genoa or Napoli, where they booked passage for the arduous sea journey to the New World.

The truth, of course, was quite different. Reality became apparent to immigrants as soon as they arrived on Ellis Island, where they were detained in densely overcrowded and unsanitary conditions. They were typically held there for many days while their papers were processed and their physical and mental health were being assessed. Many people's names were changed. It's no wonder the place became known to them as *L'Isola delle Lacrime*—the Island of Tears.

Once past the ordeal of initial processing, immigrants confronted the chaos and cultural shock of New York City, a world as far apart from the rural towns and villages of southern Italy as one could imagine. It was a world in which they were extremely vulnerable, rarely knowing the language or having the street savvy to survive. And yet they came in greater and greater numbers throughout the first decades of the new century. By 1935 there were more than 5 million Italians in America, a number of immigrants surpassed only by the Germans, who had been arriving throughout the nineteeth century. They began to settle in "Little Italys" throughout the country, although by far the greatest concentration remained in New York City.

At that time, Italians faced widespread discrimination and found little work outside menial labor. In 1910 a city official spoke candidly of why Italians were so welcome in New York: "We want someone to do the dirty work: the Irish aren't doing it any longer." The propensity of the new immigrants to undertake backbreaking work has led a distinguished American historian to write: "The greatest metropolis in the world rose from the sweat and misery of Italian labor."

And yet, of course, there is a silver, even golden, lining to the dark cloud of conditions that greeted the early Italian immigrants. As Italians throughout the twentieth century became more and more integrated into the cultural quilt that is contemporary America, they deeply influenced its culture and history, as many of the 101 chapters of this book indicate. Our food, our architecture, our music, our art, our education, our law, our politics, our sports, our films—indeed virtually every aspect of contemporary life—have been influenced by the talent, vision, and energy of the Italian immigrant spirit. That spirit is embodied in the lyrics of this anonymous "Song of the Emigrants," first published in 1881:

> In tatters, in great herds we in pain beyond belief
>   journeyed to the vast and distant land.
> Some of us did drown.
> Some of us did die of privation.
> But for every ten that perished a thousand survived
>   and endured.

All of us who are descendants of those who died, as well as those who survived and endured, take great pride in the indomitable will and courage of the Italian immigrants.

11

Italian-American Writers

The work of Italian-American writers represents a distinctive and distinguished part of American literature. Much of it is centered around the rituals of Italian family life, with its emphasis on food, family conflicts, and intensely dramatic verbal confrontations. It also captures the uniqueness of Italian-American neighborhoods, mostly in big cities like New York, Chicago, and San Francisco, where Italians settled in large numbers in the first half of the twentieth century.

Many authors have given us engaging and authentic accounts of growing up in an Italian-American family. Three of the most famous are Gay Talese, Mario Puzo, and Don DeLillo. Talese's novel *Unto the Sons* is an epic account of the Italian-American immigrant experience, chronicling several generations of an Italian family. Puzo, known primarily as the author of *The Godfather,* also wrote a number of less sensational novels, particularly *The Fortunate Pilgrim,* which tells the story of Lucia Santa, a strong and courageous woman from the mountains of southern Italy who struggles to support her family and make a life for her children in the New World. The television miniseries of the novel features Sophia Loren in the starring role.

Don DeLillo is regarded by some as one of America's greatest living writers. A substantial chunk of his encyclopedic 1997 novel, *Underworld,* deals with recollections of his upbringing on Arthur Avenue, the Italian-American section of the Bronx famous for its great delis, markets, and restaurants. His other books—*Americana, End Zone, Great Jones Street, White Noise, Libra, Mao II*—are chronicles of contemporary culture that hold a mirror up to our lives to show us how we live. *Underworld* is the most comprehensive of these, but it is also DeLillo's most personal book, capturing with great precision the experience of growing up Italian American in New York in the 1950s. Here is DeLillo, for example, describing the centrality of food in Italian-American family life: "This food, this family meal, this meat sauce simmering in a big pot with sausage and spareribs and onions and garlic, this was their loyalty and bond and well-being, and the aroma was in the halls for Rosemary to smell when she climbed the flights, rolled beef, meatballs, basil, and the savor had an irony that was painful."

Other writers, like John Fante ("Odyssey of a Wop,") Pietro di Donato *(Christ in Concrete),* Helen Barolini *(Umbertina),* Barbara Grizzuti Harrison *(Italian Days),* and Frank Lentriccchia *(Edge of Night),* although less famous, provide additional glimpses into Italian American life.

In addition to novelists and nonfiction writers, Italian-American poets have made important contributions to the American literary record. In 1925, an Italian immigrant poet named Emanuel Carnevali made a substantial impact in avant-garde poetic circles with the publication of *Tales of a Hurried Man*. Later in the century, the poet John Ciardi became an extremely influential literary figure as an editor of the *Saturday Review* and as a great "popularizer" of poetry in America. His translations of Dante's *Inferno* and *Purgatorio* became the standard texts of those works for several generations of English-speaking readers. The poets Gregory Corso and Diane di Prima added an Italian-American accent to the poetry of the "beat" generation; more recently, poets like David Citino, W. S. Di Piero, Kim Addonizio, Dana Gioia, and others have continued to illuminate aspects of Italian-American life in their work.

These writers and many others like them remind us anew that American literature is a rich, multicultural tapestry that expresses the diverse heritage of Americans of all backgrounds. Italians can take particular pride in their contribution to this amazing legacy.

12

Italian Jews

Italy has a long and proud Jewish heritage. Jews were among the first inhabitants along the Tiber River. Since the earliest days of the Roman Empire, Jews lived in and around Rome, and today the city continues to be the heart of Italian Judaism. There are approximately thirty thousand Jews in Italy, centered mostly around Rome and Milan.

In the earliest days of Venice, many Jews lived on the lagoon as traders and bankers and were part of the seafaring economy. In 1516, Jews were forced to move to a small island, which became known as the Getto Nuovo, from which the word "ghetto" derived. Cramped together in tiny quarters with limited social and economic activities, the Jews in the ghetto bonded together. All of the major cities had their ghettos, where, for a time, Jews were forced to live but were allowed to practice their religion without interference.

When Napoleon's regime swept through the region, igniting the fires of Italian liberty, Jews were freed from the ghettos and allowed to live where they pleased. After Napoleon's fall, many voices still cried out for Jewish liberty. In Turin, King Carlo Alberto officially emancipated them on March 19, 1848. Subsequently, many became involved in the cause of Italian unification. Issac Artom, secretary to one of the Italian founding fathers Camillo Cavour, was Jewish, as was Giacomo Dina, the publisher of Cavour's newspaper *Il Risorgimento.*

Because Jews have been active in every segment of Italian society, their culture has been completely assimilated. If you think Italian food is good, try Italian-*Jewish* food, with its own special take on meatballs and caponata.

During Mussolini's Fascist regime, Jews were persecuted once again, and many of them were carted off to Germany to become victims of the Holocaust. But many heroic Italians came to the aid of Jewish neighbors, hiding them from the Nazis. After the war, the Italian Jews raised their synagogues from the rubble and rebuilt their communities in harmony with the rest of the battered nation. Author Primo Levi has chronicled the Jewish-Italian experience of the era in several novels. Vittorio De Sica directed *the Garden of the Finzi-Continis* (1970), a drama about Italian Jews during the war, which won an Oscar for Best Foreign Film of that year.

While most people associate Italians with Catholicism because of the presence of the pope in Vatican City and because the vast majority of Italians are Catholic, the Italian Jewish legacy is unique and enduring.

13

La Lingua Italiana

La lingua Italiana is anything but an ordinary language. Speak in any other tongue and you are merely communicating. Speak Italian and the conversation lives and breathes with its own dynamic vitality. It is a language where the vowels and consonants perform a rhapsodic dance together—a passionate, musical language of love.

It is a food. We all know how Italians love a good meal, and this desire spills into the words. Reading a menu or a cookbook is a delicious exercise for the jaw and lips. Tortellini, gnocchi, aglio e olio, prosciutto. The words float on the tongue. Lasagna, ravioli, pesce. The mandible moves as if chewing. Cannoli, gelati, tirami sú. The mouth waters as a lubricant for the alphabet. Speaking of this rich food is the antipasto to the antipasto. And it extends to all words, not just those centered around the table. A light conversation is a snack; an intense one, a full-blown dinner. To talk is to eat is to enjoy.

It is a song. Hearing someone speak Italian from a distance is like hearing a familiar tune on the radio. It has melody, rhythm. The inflection is up, and then it is down. The tone is clear, delicate. An Italian day begins and ends with this music. A crisp, perky *Buon giorno* is on everyone's lips in the morning. When the night falls, a gentle *Buona sera* is the greeting, the sera lingering a beat longer on the palette, letting you ponder the hours in between.

It is a dance. The rhythm is too strong, the melody too sweet. The head must move with the syllables, and the body cannot help but follow. The hand cups at the fingertip; the wrist becomes limp. It rocks back and forth in gentle cadence with the meter. (See chapter 8, "Hand Gestures.")

It is a wine. The language has gracefully aged through the centuries into a full-bodied form of expression. It has a bouquet. The patter of phrases often tickles the nose. It is smooth and robust. It often leaves you light-headed, intoxicated with terminology. Of course, it's romantic. It's a Romance language. Examine the root and you have Roma.

Like a rose, it, too, has its thorns. Cross an Italian and all the food, wine, song, and dance come hurling at you. The meal turns, the song screeches, the fists rise, the wine brings nausea. There is simply no defense.

All the magic of Italy is contained within its wonderful language. One sentence can send you to heaven or hell. Purgatory is reserved for those who do not understand it.

14

Leaning Tower of Pisa

It's one of the most beautiful goofs in all of history. The bell tower, aptly located in the Campo dei Miracoli (Field of Miracles) in Pisa, Italy, is a stunning monument to the human will, a structure that literally struggled to be built.

On August 9, 1173, architect Bonanno Pisano began construction of the bell tower in the center of the square. A little over two years later, during the building of the third tier, its trademark lean was initially discovered. It wasn't the fault of the design—the cylindrical measurements attest to its architect's integrity—but the soil on which the tower was situated was too soft, and the tower's foundation tipped. This naturally posed a dilemma, and for ninety years the tower remained incomplete.

There must be something about the way it inclined that intrigued the Pisans. They attempted to straighten it, but after a few years of trying, they realized it was impossible. However, that didn't stop

completion of the tower. Giovanni di Simone took over the project, and four *loggette* (stories) were added, stopping whenever war broke out in the volatile region. The belfry, residing on the seventh and final level, is attributed to one of Pisano's relatives, who completed the tower in 1350, 175 years after its flaw was first discovered.

And there it stands, or *leans,* gently falling toward earth in what might be called the most elegant display of the law of gravity ever. The graceful, rounded façades of the "Little Tower That Could" are beautiful, but it is its lean—the force of nature tipping the scales—that makes it truly special. Recent attempts to shore up the tower have had mixed results. Although nobody wants it to be straight, no one wants it to fall, either. Six hundred tons of lead were added to the north side of the foundation in 1994, and for a brief moment time stopped. Much to everyone's horror, the tower actually began to straighten! But one night in September that very next year, Mother Nature again slipped in her slender finger, and the tower shifted 2.5 millimeters southward overnight.

No one knows when or if it will finally fall to earth. Right now it is poised like an elegant ballerina before her final bow. Considered one of the modern wonders of the world, this is one "failure" of which Italians can truly be proud.

15

Mona Lisa

What is it about the smile that Leonardo da Vinci captured on the face of his portrait of Lisa di Antonio Maria Gherardini that has enchanted viewers of his painting for over five hundred years? The Mona Lisa is exhibited behind glass in its own room at the Louvre in Paris, where throngs of visitors march past it every day, watching her eyes follow theirs as they leave the room, their momentary encounter with the world's most famous painting behind them.

Leonardo painted the portrait over a period of three years, between 1503 and 1506, when his model was in her mid-twenties and he was in his fifties. Of course, in the painting she is ageless and timeless. She sits, hands crossed, one lightly touching the other, against a backdrop of rocks and overcast sky. Her dark hair, parted in the center, falls easily over both of her shoulders. A winding road disappears into the rocks behind her right shoulder. A small bridge crosses a ravine behind her left. These details only magnify her human presence, which dominates the landscape. This is a portrait of the High Renaissance, where humanity is the measure of all things.

Her penetrating gaze transfixes us with its encyclopedia of contradictions: It is seductive and distancing, happy and sorrowful, filled with both amusement and regret, hope and loss, pain and pleasure. These dualities are expressed as well in the enigmatic smile that bespeaks a knowingness beyond the artist's ability to explain it. The smile that has occasioned so much commentary and inspired so many artists and writers captures the soul of a woman in all of her conflicting personages—mother, daughter, sister, wife, lover. The Mona Lisa is all of these, embodied in a single woman who refuses to be categorized and therefore limited by any one of these roles.

This transcendence perhaps explains why reproductions of the painting are among the most defaced and vandalized images in all of art. She has appeared with horns, hundreds of varieties of mustaches, beards, whiskers, eyeglasses, freckles, pimples, and as many other alterations of the human face one can imagine. You can find pictures of her winking, scowling, sticking out her tongue, and doing all sorts of other things intended to parody her perfection. But that perfection and that wholeness cannot be denied. It was captured forever by a great Italian artist who gave this gift of womanly essence to the world.

16

Murano Glass

Murano glass is as beautiful as it is delicate, as mysterious as it is transparent. Glass and the art of glassmaking have always been a source of fascination to human beings: How can a substance such as sand, when heated, turn solid and opaque? Put science, ritual, and art together and you have the essence of this golden craft.

For over a thousand years the tiny island of Murano, near Venice, has been home to the alchemy of glassmaking.

An important port for centuries, the region has been a meeting place for artisans from around the world to hone their skills by becoming involved in the production of Vetri Murano, the most delicate and beautiful glass produced in Europe.

With the threat of fire looming large in the wooden houses of early Venice, the glassblowing furnaces, which generate intense heat, were all moved to Murano, where fire could be more easily contained. From this relocation, a camaraderie, kinship, and a kind of semireligion developed around the making of crystal and glass objects.

They don't just make glass in Murano. They blow it, they fire it, they stamp it, they engrave it, they paint it, they shape it from pastes, they dye it different colors, they twist it, they garnish it. Each has its own special history, its own secret recipe, and a devoted group of artisans.

There's the *làttimo,* a milk-white glass with an appearance similar to porcelain that has been a favorite since the mid-fifteenth century. Or *ghiaccio,* an "ice glass" that appears like a cracked glacier, the effect achieved by dipping it into water during the creative process. There's even *avventurina,* a highly difficult way of making glass paste; its name, which, translated, means "adventurous," gives some idea of the risks involved in making it.

Most innovations in the field can be traced back to Murano and its glassmakers. Angelo Barovier, who is credited with the invention of làttimo, also perfected the first purified crystal glass, which ushered in a new era in glassmaking. In an age of high-tech machinery, glassmaking is one of the few crafts where the work is still done hands (and lips) on. Today its legacy continues to grow as some of the finest Italian artisans practice the tradition handed down for generations over the fiery ovens of Murano.

17

Opera

Opera is the music of Italy's soul. It originated in Florence during the Renaissance when a group of musicians and philosophers, called the Florentine *camerata* (meaning "friend" or "society"), revived Greek drama, adding a musical line to the development of the plot. They called this musical rendition of the dramatic story the recitativo. In the early seventeenth century, the first great Italian opera composer, Claudio Monteverdi, added the idea of melodic songs, called arias, that the characters in the play, rather than the chorus, would actually sing. These two elements, combined with elaborate scenery and costumes, formed the basis of opera as we know it today.

Italian operas were of two types—opera seria, or serious opera usually based on classical myths; and opera buffa, or comic opera, which began as comic relief to be played and sung during the intermissions of an opera seria. In 1778 the crown jewel of Italian opera theaters, La Scala, opened in Milan with a production of Antonio

Salieri's *Europa Riconosciuta*. Despite having been bombed in World War II, La Scala remains the premier opera venue in the world today, and no diva or great tenor can be said to have truly arrived on the opera scene until he or she has sung there.

Italian opera flourished and blossomed in the nineteenth century, stimulated by work of the great composers Vincenzo Bellini, Gaetano Donizetti, Giacomo Puccini, Gioacchino Rossini, and of course, the great Giuseppe Verdi (see chapter 74). Together, these musical geniuses established the classical repertoire of Italian opera, giving us works like *Norma* and *La Sonnambula* (Bellini); *La Bohème*, *Madama Butterfly*, and *Tosca* (Puccini); *Lucia di Lammermoor* and *Don Pasquale* (Donizetti); *Il Barbiere de Seviglia*, *Guillaume Tell* (Rossini) and *Aida*, *La Traviata*, *Rigoletto*, and *Otello* (Verdi). These works continue to be performed throughout the world, and their melodies are familiar to music lovers everywhere. Rossini's famous "William Tell Overture" has become popular in America because it was the theme of the radio and television drama *The Lone Ranger* of the forties and fifties.

In the United States, the art of the opera was revitalized again by an Italian named Gian-Carlo Menotti. He was born in Cadegliano, Italy, and began writing librettos at the age of ten. He came to America in 1927, and his career flourished. His most famous works, *The Medium*, *The Consul*, and *Ahmal and the Night Visitors*, established an American opera tradition for modern times.

Opera is about passion, drama, and emotion. Its themes of betrayal, love, death, and intrigue are universal but heightened by the larger-than-life spectacle that a full-blown opera performance presents. The story line, the costumes, the settings, the full orchestral accompaniment to the great tenors, sopranos, and other singers on the stage, all combine to give us the first truly multimedia art form. And it's not surprising, of course, that something so dramatic, emotional, and intense was born in Italy.

18

Pinocchio

It's one of the best-loved fables in the world. The story of a talking piece of wood that is carved into a puppet has enchanted generations of children and adults everywhere.

Carlo Lorenzini was a nineteenth-century Florentine author and journalist who wrote under the psuedonym Collodi. Having had some success translating French fairy tales, Collodi decided to try his hand at writing his own children's story. The result was a "bit of foolishness" he sent to his friend in Rome, who was the editor of *Il Giornale dei Bambini,* a newspaper for children. The editor loved it and published the first chapter in July 1881. The response was immediate and overwhelming. The story, which had first been titled simply *Storia di un Burattino (The Story of a Puppet)* was transformed into *Le Avventure di Pinocchio (The Adventures of Pinocchio)* and became a regular serial in the newspaper, with eager young readers awaiting each new chapter.

When chapter fifteen had Pinocchio killed by assassins, the public was horrified. There was such an outcry that Collodi decided to continue his serial and saved poor Pinocchio in a subsequent installment. In 1883 the entire story was published as one book that later became an integral part of every Italian's childhood.

The book was translated into many languages, including English. A young man named Walt Disney discovered the story and turned it into the animated classic *Pinocchio* (1940) that most Americans are familiar with today. The film contains many of Pinocchio's adventures, including his being changed into a donkey, swallowed by a whale (a shark in the book), and finally transformed into a real boy, but the Disney version lacks the passion of Collodi's original story.

Pinocchio is truly one of literature's underdogs: a hungry puppet-boy who causes mischief wherever he travels, learning the hardships of life and the importance of family and friends. He triumphs when he becomes "real" at the end of his journey. Its popularity in the 1880s, as young Italy was taking its first steps toward becoming a "real" nation, is no accident. Along with *The Divine Comedy* (see chapter 52) and *The Prince* (see chapter 62), it is one of Italy's most prestigious literary artifacts, studied and written about by scholars all over the world. But you don't need to have a degree to enjoy the story as Collodi wrote it. All it takes is a heart.

19

Popular Music

Italians are born entertainers. Whether it's in the kitchen, on the front porch, or at Carnegie Hall, entertaining is a natural extension of the Italian passion for life. The substantial and ongoing contribution by Italians to American popular music is another source of pride. Here are just a few of the very best:

Dean Martin, born Dino Tony Crocetti, was a class act. A member of the illustrious Rat Pack, with *paisani* Sammy Davis Jr. and Frank Sinatra, he was the wild card in the Vegas deck—a lady's man, a gambler, a drinker. Ordinarily, these would be considered unflattering traits, but Martin wore the suit with style. Always a wisecracker, he would often pull pranks in the middle of the concerts with his pals, even stealing the show from the great Sinatra with his charm. As an actor, he was one of the best straight men ever. His seventeen films with Jerry Lewis are comedy classics. And Martin infused American popular music with songs that had a distinctly Italian flavor—like "That's Amore," "Oh

Marie," "Volare," "On an Evening in Roma," "In Napoli," and many others.

Henry Mancini was another icon of popular music culture. Between 1958 and 1964, he was the king of music for Hollywood films and television. Think of *Peter Gunn* or the *Pink Panther* and you can't help but hum one of Mancini's memorable themes. "Moon River," "Days of Wine and Roses," and "The Baby Elephant Walk," are further testament to his ability to evoke strong emotions with his melodies. All in all, he won twenty Grammys, had seven gold records, and garnered four Oscars for his work.

Louis Prima, a.k.a. "the Wildest," was the true essence of the Italian celebrative spirit. With his raspy rumble, hilarious lyrical improvisations, and raucous trumpet playing (earning him his other nickname, "the Lip"), Prima made his audiences grin from ear to ear. With his wife Keely Smith's silky vocals and deadpan style complementing his rough voice and clowning antics, he was the toast of the Las Vegas strip from the 1950s to the early 1960s. A Sicilian by descent, he is forever immortalized as the voice of King Louie the Orangutan, singing "I Wanna Walk Like You" in Disney's *The Jungle Book* (1967).

And what tribute to Italian popular singers would be complete without mentioning the incomparable talents of Tony Bennett? In voice and phrasing he ranks second only to Sinatra. With memorable interpretations of such classics as "I Left My Heart in San Francisco" and

"Because of You," Bennett's voice is always evocative of a heightened emotional state. And he's the only singer of his era to truly cross the generation gap by having an extraordinarily successful concert on *MTV Unplugged*, winning him a Grammy and legions of new pierced and tattooed young fans.

Music is a passion deep within the soul of every proud Italian. Listening to these artists stirs that passion in each of us.

20

Proverbs

Although many Italians can carry on long, involved conversations with constant gesturing and passion, Italian proverbs cut to the chase. Often individuals in a family are identified with particular proverbs. A father who is an especially patient person goes around saying, *"Pazienza e fortitudine,"* ("Patience and fortitude"), extolling them as virtues to which everyone should aspire. A person who despises dishonesty will tell you, *"La bugia ha le gambe corte"* ("A lie has short legs"), meaning it won't get you very far.

Some Italian proverbs are unusually economical. Whereas the English version tells us, "No sooner said that done," the Italians give us the very soul of brevity: *"Detto, fatto."* ("Said, done.") And whereas we say, "Out of sight, out of mind," the Italians speak of the heart rather than the mind: *"Lontano dagli occhi, lontano dal cuore."* ("What is far from the eyes is far from the heart.")

Italian proverbs tend to be passed on in families from one generation to the next. Here is a list of proverbial expressions that have been passed down in our family. Grandpa Moramarco wrote them long ago in his distinctive handwriting on a piece of paper that is something of a family treasure. We provide both the Italian and a rough English equivalent because some are not easily translatable:

Chi va piano va sano e va lontano.
Who goes slowly goes in good health and travels far.

Chi la dura la vince.
Survivors are winners.

Chi in alto va cade precipitevolissimevolmente.
The higher you climb, the faster you fall.

Il mondo è fatto a scale: c 'é chi scende e c 'é chi sale.
The world is made of stairs: some climb and some descend.

Chi va per ingannare resta ingannato.
Whoever intends to deceive winds up deceived.

L'ozio é padrone dei vizi.
Laziness is the landlord of vices.

*Nessuno conosce che cosa sta cucinando nella vaschetta meglio di chi
    fa la mescolatura.*
No one knows what is cooking in the pan better than the one
    doing the stirring.

21

Resistance to Fascism

The rise of fascism in Italy under dictator Benito "Il Duce" Mussolini marks Italy's darkest period. Why include it in a book about Italian pride? Mussolini and his Black Shirt brigade remind us that pride can also be considered one of the seven deadly sins.

It is one thing to love your heritage, yourself, and your country. But when these feelings lead to the humiliation, persecution, and death of other human beings, it is shameful and wrong. Mussolini's regime was pride at its worst.

Taking advantage of a young, impoverished nation at the end of . World War I, Mussolini deceived Italians with his charismatic speech and ways. The Fascist Party started out small, getting only 7 percent of the total vote in the 1921 elections. But it grew rapidly and zealously as Mussolini's thirst for grandeur and power amassed tens of thousands of followers. The rapid growth of fascism lead to a march on Rome in

October 1922, when Mussolini was commissioned to form a government by King Vittorio Emanuele III.

Mussolini's rule was total. He jailed, expelled, and killed those who did not believe in his ways. He was particularly rigid about the participation of women in political affairs. "Women do not count," il Duce said, and he attempted to curtail their contribution to society, except for being wives and mothers. Rapidly he transformed Italy from an independent constitutional monarchy to a totalitarian state.

But many resisted, and women particularly were horrified by the brutality of the Fascists. Many refused to submit to Mussolini's propaganda. Instead, they enrolled in universities and took jobs despite his attempt to ostracize them. Some women writers appeared on the cultural page of major newspapers, writing personal stories that empowered females, giving them a voice in this faceless regime. Robin Pickering-Iazzi, in her book *Unspeakable Women*, translates works by authors such as Grazia Deledda (who won the Nobel Prize in Literature in 1926) and Ada Negri, shedding new light on the feelings of women during this period.

When Mussolini did the unthinkable and allied himself with Hitler in World War II, many Italians helped their Jewish comrades reach Switzerland, where they would be safe from the concentration camps. Because of this, only 10 percent of Italian Jews were killed, fewer than in any Nazi-occupied country. This fact doesn't mitigate the horrors of the Holocaust, but it does underscore the courage of those who resisted the Fascist regime.

Italy's entry into the war was a total disaster. Hundreds of thousands of people were killed, and what popularity Mussolini had up until then vanished. On July 25, 1943, Mussolini, having lost the support of the people, was arrested by the king, and Italy joined the Allies.

Il Duce managed to escape for a time to northern Italy, where he ran a puppet government for the Germans in the final years of the war. But the anti-Fascist movement grew stronger, and a group of rebels, called the *partigiani* (partisans), formed the Resistance, which fought against *both* Mussolini's army and the Nazis. Mussolini, knowing his days were numbered, tried to escape the country disguised as a soldier. The partigiani discovered him and shot him, his mistress, and several of his cohorts. In order to show their disgust with the way he destroyed the fabric of the country, the partigiani hung Mussolini and his mistress, Clara Petacci, by their feet in a public square in Milan.

Unfortunately, the grim specter of fascism still rears its ugly head. In Bologna, right-wing terrorists planted a bomb in the train station in 1980, killing two hundred people. A monument resides there commemorating the men and women who fought and continue to fight against the worst kind of pride there is.

22

The Roman Calendar

Sometimes Italians themselves are surprised by the influence the inhabitants of their narrow, boot-shaped peninsula have had on the ways of the world. Consider the calendar by which we measure the days of the week, the months of the year, and the years of the centuries. Calendars make it possible for us to keep a record of the past and make plans for the future. Without them we are stranded in an eternal present, where there is no history and there can be no dreams.

The ancient Egyptians made the remarkable discovery that a year was divided seasonally and could be measured from the shortest day of the year to the next occurrence of the shortest day. They devised a calendar of 365 days divided into three seasons of four months each: winter, spring, and summer. From Persia, the Egyptians got the idea of naming the months. Had the Egyptian calendar prevailed, we would be talking about *Thoth, Tybi,* and *Pachons* instead of January, February, and March.

But of course the Egyptian calendar did not prevail. At about the same time the Egyptian calendar was established, across the Mediterranean a legendary prerepublic ruler by the name of Numa Pompilius was devising an almanac. He named the months according to some of the Roman deities (Janus, Mars, and Juno, for example) and others according to their numerical occurrence during the year (September, October, November, December—in Numa's calendar the year began in March, so these were the seventh, eighth, ninth and tenth months). Later, the months of July and August (Quintilis and Sextilis in Numa's calendar) were named after Julius and Augustus Caesar.

In the early days of the Roman Empire, the calendar was observed haphazardly and perpetuated many irregularities. In the first century B.C., the Roman astronomer Sosigenes advised the emperor Julius Caesar that important modifications had to be made to standardize the calendar and regularize the position of the seasons. Because of the nonobservance of leap years and other astronomical realities in the centuries intervening between Numa and Caesar, January was now occurring in autumn! The Julian calendar, later slightly modified by Pope Gregory in the sixteenth century, became the prototype of the calendar you carry around with you in your daytimer. So the next time you jot down an appointment for July 5 or August 3, for example, think of Julius and Augustus Caesar and how Rome's great legacy still organizes our lives today.

23

Scientists

There are many noteworthy examples of Italian genius in the sciences.

We can thank Guglielmo Marconi for inventing the radio. In 1895, at the ripe young age of twenty-one, Marconi made a remarkable discovery. A student at the University of Bologna, he created a wireless means of sending telegraph signals. Later, Marconi moved to England and established a communication system of nine miles; in 1901 he received signals from across the Atlantic. For his distinguished achievements, Marconi won the Nobel Prize in physics in 1909.

Count Alessandro Giuseppe Antonio Anastasio Volta is responsible for major innovations in electrochemistry. His creation of the voltaic pile was the precursor of the modern battery. He also invented the electrophorus, a charge-accumulating machine that became the model for the electric condenser. As a tribute to his revolutionary work, the term *volt* is used as a measuring device for electric current.

Antonio Meucci is one of the most fascinating characters of

modern science. Using electromagnetic impulses in the body, he developed an astounding way to stimulate tissue growth and cure common ills. He would give a patient a copper wire to place in his or her mouth and a copper rod to hold in one hand. Next, he would go into the other room, grab the wires in a similar fashion, and run a tiny current. Naturally, this unique method of medical treatment sometimes caused a bit of squeamishness in his patients. One day he was treating a man for migraine headaches. Startled by the small current he felt in his body, the man screamed. Meucci, in the other room, "felt" the scream in his mouth. The sound had been carried over the wires! Meucci spent many years developing the "teletrophone," an acoustic telephony system that predated Alexander Graham Bell's inventions by decades. A man of the sea, he used this invention as a way for ships to communicate and navigate through a series of tones and developed several prototypes for the early telephone. The latter years of his life were spent trying to defend in court his rightful claim to the concepts he developed against the emerging telephone monopolies. A poor Italian immigrant was no match for the Bell Telephone Company, and he died in obscurity.

Today's labs are also filled with pioneering Italian scientists. Rita Levi-Montalcini has been researching nerve damage for more than fifty years. In 1986, she won a Nobel Prize for her studies. Carlo Rubbia is known for helping discover subatomic particles and received his Nobel Prize in 1984.

There is no area of modern science that has not been affected by the inventions of Italians. From the Renaissance and before to the present day and beyond, Italians have been, and will continue to be, at the forefront of new ideas that change the world.

24

Shroud of Turin

Catholics have always cherished physical items that are associated with saints or with Jesus Christ Himself. They call these items relics, and one of Christianity's most sacred and controversial is the Shroud of Turin. On this fragile yellowed cloth there is a life-size image of a bearded man who appears to have wounds on his hands and feet, around his head, in his side, and on his back. Is this the actual imprint of Jesus? Many Christians believe it is, but the authenticity of the relic is hotly contested.

The actual history only goes as far back as 1203, when French crusader Robert de Clari describes seeing the shroud in Constantinople. Its first documented appearance, however, did not occur until 1353 in Lirey, France, and since 1578 the shroud has been housed in the Duomo di San Giovanni in Turin and has remained there almost continuously ever since.

Displayed openly only a few times each century, the shroud is truly awe-inspiring. What is most remarkable is that the image appears to be a photographic negative of a human form. A recent carbon testing has placed its origin at around the year 1325, but the accuracy of those tests is open to debate. If it is a fraud, there is still no explanation as to how the image could have been created by medieval forgers who knew nothing about modern photographic techniques. All tests have failed to duplicate the imprint of the bleeding, wounded man that appears so realistically on this linen.

The shroud continues to be an object of fascination to the faithful and skeptical alike who want to peer at this mysterious imprint. It has become the single most examined relic in human history, and the public's reverence for its shows no signs of abating. At the last public display of the shroud in this century, in 1998, four thousand visitors an hour paid their respects.

Whether the actual image of Christ or a clever fabrication, this artifact makes an indelible impression on those lucky enough to view the real thing in person. And to do that, you've got to go to the wonderful Italian city of Turin.

25

Soccer (*Calcio*)

It is Italy's national pastime. Whenever the local team is playing, you can be sure that it is to a full house. On Sundays, all eyes are on the television set to watch the latest and greatest battle it out in the open-air stadiums. If you're in town during a World Cup or a final, you can forget about going anywhere or doing anything that doesn't involve *calcio, calcio, calcio!*

Although modern soccer, or football, as its known to the rest of the world, has its origins in Britain, one can trace versions from Italy. *Harpastan* was a game Julius Caesar had his troops play. One ball would be thrown out to five hundred men who would then fight over it. The last one standing was declared the winner. In the Renaissance, the Florentines had their own version, which was just as vigorous. Every year, Florence relives these glory days in June with the Calcio Storico, a no-holds-barred game with a wooden ball and the players in period costumes battling it out on a mud-filled field.

Soccer is one of the most physically challenging sports in the world. The game, which involves two teams of eleven people, is one of almost constant motion as the players relay the ball across the field and back, using every part of their body except their hands. Only the goalie of each team is allowed to grab the ball to prevent the opposing team from scoring. There is rarely a time-out, and no downs or innings. The game is comprised of two 45-minute halves, and the action is nonstop.

Theoretically, it is a very simple game. You only need a ball, an empty space, and two goal areas. Therefore, it is a game that every Italian can play without expensive equipment or gymnasiums, which those living in the poorer neighborhoods of Italian cities usually lack. Consequently, soccer has become intertwined with the social rituals of all regions and classes. From the yards and streets have come the heroes of the Italian soccer world.

Italian leagues began forming at the end of the nineteenth century and have been in full force ever since. The ancient feuds that kept the peninsula from becoming a united nation until the late 1800s have their new battleground on the playing field. Here Siena and Florence rekindle old grudges, and the Roman Empire rises or falls with the scoring of goals.

Since the 1930s, soccer fans have had the World Cup, a contest pitting country against country every four years. Italy has always placed high in the rankings and has won three of the cups to date. And there's no question that Italians are very proud of that!

26

Style and Fashion

The Italian dress code is the blueprint for all things fashionable. It is an outward manifestation of Italian pride. Walk along the shopping boulevards of Rome or Milan and you will see men and women dressed in the eye-catching apparel of Valentino, Versace, Armani, Gucci, and the whole squadron of Italian designers who have revolutionized the fashion world. These designers have given us the impression that an Italian leaves behind an unmistakable imprint of elegance and class on everything he or she touches.

Italians have been influencing style and fashion for hundreds of years. Wool, linen, silk, and other exotic cloths have always been a part of the general "fabric" of Italian identity. The silk trade blossomed around Lake Como in the tenth century, and the art of shoemaking began in Venice in the twelfth.

The birthday of modern Italian fashion might be said to be February 12, 1951. On that day a Florentine by the name of Giovanni Battista

Giorgini put together a fashion show of some of the best Italian designers of the era. This was the world's first real glimpse of a total look that centered around Italian stylists, and the fashion industry went absolutely mad.

Hollywood made famous the Fontana sisters, who designed dresses for Ava Gardner. Maiuccia Mandelli, a former schoolteacher, launched the Krizia line in 1959, which became instantly popular worldwide. From then on, Milan would be the center of Italian fashion.

One of the most influential designers, Giorgio Armani, got his start there, first as a window dresser and a buyer. His sexy suits for *American Gigolo* (1980) and playful, baggy look for *Annie Hall* (1977) established him as *the* designer for the era, and his line of clothing continues to be a watermark in fashion to this day.

Gianni Versace is another world-renowned name. His dramatic, romantic, and flamboyant ensembles stunned and enthralled the fashion-conscious throughout his fifteen-year career as designer extraordinaire. His life ended tragically when, at the height of his career, he was murdered by a demented serial killer in 1997. The company continues, with his creative spirit still at the helm.

Fashion runways are always crowded with Italian designs. Valentino, Capucci, and Fendi aren't just names; they're statements, symbols, monuments to good taste. Gucci, Ferré, Biagotti—textile dreams wrapped around stars, starlets, and supermodels. The styles, from blacks to shocking pinks, baggy clothing to skin-tight, ultralong to ultramini, are all over the fashion map. What unites these visionaries is the Italian blood that pulses through their veins and "spills" into their creations.

Nowadays you can't turn on the television, walk through a shopping mall, or open a fashion magazine without seeing the handiwork of Italian designers. They are the envy of the world, for even if you can't be an Italian, at least you can dress like one.

27

Trials of the Mafiosi

A cancer has been growing within the Italian community for hundreds of years, and its name is the Cosa Nostra (literally "Our Thing"). The Mafia, as it is more commonly known, is a group of close-knit criminals who control the trafficking of drugs, money, weapons, gambling, and anything else that is profitable, even if illegal or immoral.

Its development dates back to the Middle Ages in Sicily when landowners hired ruffians to police their neighborhoods in the absence of a central government. As time passed, these groups broadened their bases and tightened their ranks. After the devastation of World War II, the Mafia was literally the only organized governing body left in Sicily, and it worked closely with the Allies to restore order. But the mafiosi weren't interested in the good of the people.

Over the years following the war, the Mafia seeped into many areas of Italian government and business, funneling money away from worthy projects. Sicily and southern Italy suffered the worst.

As of late, however, both Italy and the United States have had some success in ridding their societies of the criminal element. In Italy in the 1990s, a wave of reform swept the entire political system, and once-untouchable leaders were dragged into courtrooms. In the 1992 maxi-trial in Palermo, where a special courtroom was created, three hundred mafiosi were sentenced to prison. The Cosa Nostra fought back, assassinating prosecutor Giovanni Falcone, his wife, and others who threatened their iron grip, but their plan backfired. The hearts of the public went out to the victims, who became martyrs for a larger movement. All across Italy, former members began saying, "*Basta,*" to organized crime. The *pentiti* (penitents) stepped into the courtrooms to finger their former bosses in hopes of ending their chokehold on society once and for all.

In America, New York mob boss John Gotti was put behind bars, thanks in part to Sammy "the Bull" Gravano, a confidant of Gotti's who risked his life by breaking the Mafia "code of silence" to help the FBI bring Gotti to justice. As a result, the New York Mafia was dealt a severe blow.

Organized crime is prevalent in many countries and among many ethnic groups, but Italians are singled out as stereotypical mobsters. Let us take a moment here to express pride in those Italian men and women who have stood up for justice in fighting the ongoing war against Mob rule.

28

Unification of Italy

Although there have been centuries of great Italians and wonderful cities, the nation of Italy is in fact younger than the United States. It took the vision of many dedicated Italians to realize a unified republic, and these "founding fathers" are an important part of Italian cultural identity.

Until the late nineteenth century, the regions of Italy were ruled by monarchs, foreigners, lords, or popes. Italy was the battleground of wars between the French, Spanish, English, and Austrians. The Italian people had no voice in their own destiny.

It wasn't until the late eighteenth century that the peninsula began to be viewed as a single political entity. Ironically, it was a Frenchman, Napoleon—whose true ancestry was Italian—who first succeeded in creating the Kingdom of Italy, with himself as its leader. Napoleon's kingdom did not last long. When his forces were defeated in 1815, the old kings and dukes marched back to their thrones, and the country was carved up once again. But the seeds of unification had been planted, and the idea of an Italian nation began to blossom.

The years 1815–61 are known as the Risorgimento, a "reawakening" of Italian nationalism. A rebel militia was formed called the Carbonari—named after black coal because it burns with a fiery heat inside, signifying both the group's underground status and their revolutionary fervor. One prominent member, Giuseppe Mazzini, was arrested in 1830 and exiled for his role in the Genoa uprising. In Paris, he formed a group called Young Italy and wrote "open letters" to influential Italians, arguing for a unified nation.

Others followed his lead. Vincenzo Gioberti wrote "The Moral and Civil Supremacy of the Italians," and Cesare Balbo penned "Italy's Hopes." Poet Giacormo Leopardi mused over patriotism, and the operas of Rossini and Verdi were filled with the nationalist spirit. Suddenly, Italian pride was everywhere.

All that was needed was action, and the three leaders who emerged to finally bring all of Italy under one flag were King Vittorio Emanuele II of Piedmont; Count Camillo Cavour, his diplomat; and Guiseppe Garibaldi, a general who is the true hero of the Italian nation.

Cavour, knowing Piedmont needed an ally in its war against Austria, befriended the French leader Louis Napoleon. In 1859, Piedmont joined forces with the French to defeat the Austro-Hungarians in Lombardy and annexed the region. But no one expected what followed: Tuscany, Parma, Modena, and Bologna revolted against their rulers and asked to be absorbed by Piedmont as well. King Vittorio now ruled the upper north.

It all happened rather quickly after that. Garibaldi was put in charge of the Mille, a group of one thousand volunteer groups, to restore order in Sicily, which was rebelling against the king of Naples. A charismatic leader, he landed on the shores of the island and within a month had the whole region under his control. Garibaldi set sail back to the mainland, conquered the entire south, and headed toward Rome.

Cavour, who never trusted Garibaldi, convinced King Vittorio to meet the Mille before they reached Rome in case Garibaldi had desires of taking the country for himself. On the way, Vittorio's army annexed the remaining papal states, placing him in charge of the entire northern half of the peninsula. On October 26, 1860, the two men met face-to-face near Teano. But instead of provoking bloodshed, Garibaldi greeted his sovereign with the words that proclaimed Italian unity: "I salute the first king of Italy!"

By 1876 the Veneto region was acquired, and in 1870, Rome finally ceded to the new nation. A single country shaped like a boot was born. Today there is hardly a town in Italy without its Piazza Cavour, Via Garibaldi, or a monument to Vittorio Emanuele, reminding everyone of the great struggle that finally brought the country together.

29

U.S. Politics

Italians are justifiably proud of the substantial contributions they have made in the American political arena. Because the Italian-American population has been concentrated in the New York area, it is not surprising that a long legacy of political activism exists there. In 1917, Fiorello La Guardia became the first major Italian-American political figure to serve in the House of Representatives and was later elected mayor of New York in 1933. Known as "the Little Flower" (a translation of his first name) La Guardia personalized the mayor's office, becoming famous for reading the Sunday comics on the radio to the children of New York. He was so beloved that New Yorkers named an airport after him as a memorial to his integrity and dedication to the well-being of the city. The La Guardia legacy was carried on into the very end of the twentieth century with the colorful mayoralty of Rudolph Giuliani, another Italian American who is devoted to his city.

Other New Yorkers active in American politics have included the first Italian-American governor of the state, Mario Cuomo, who became an important figure in national Democratic Party politics, although he disappointed many of his followers when he declined to run for the presidency in 1992. On the other hand, Italians can be proud that the first woman to run for the vice presidency of the United States was an Italian-American congresswoman, Geraldine Ferraro, who ran on the Democratic ticket with Walter Mondale in 1984. The first woman to be elected to a state governorship was also "one of us": Ella Grasso of Connecticut.

The first Italian American to be elected to the U.S. Senate was John Pastore of Rhode Island, and he was followed by a significant number of others in all parts of the country, including Denis De Concini of Arizona, Pete Domenici of New Mexico, and Alfonse D'Amato of New York. A particularly significant contribution to American politics was made by Representative Peter Rodino of New Jersey when he chaired the House Judiciary Committee during the Nixon impeachment hearings.

Italian politicians have remained active in American government despite being stereotyped as gangsters with Mafia connections. In fact, many people suspect that the threat of such accusations figured in Mario Cuomo's decision not to run for president. It is to the great credit of the Italian political figures mentioned here that they have served their country honorably and well despite this deeply entrenched prejudice.

30

The Watts Towers

The Watts Towers is one of the most striking examples of folk architecture in the world. A collection of spires made of cement, wire, bits of pipe, steel, and other found metal objects and decorated with broken bottles, plates, and cups, it is the vision of one Italian immigrant named Simon Rodia.

Rodia began his work in 1921. For the following thirty-three years he worked alone at 1765 East 107th Street in the Watts section of Los Angeles, building his monument up from and around his home. With Italian music blaring from the Victrola, Rodia would sing along as he worked on his masterpiece in the evenings after his day job as a stone cutter. Scaling the seventy-foot-plus towers with a window-washer's belt, a bucket of seashells, and a smile, he would inlay the pieces by hand into a grand mosaic. He called the piece *Our Town,* and saw it as his homage to the city of Los Angeles and the country of America.

It was truly a labor of love. Of course, his neighbors thought he was crazy, building this cathedral-like structure of cement and wire in the middle of the immigrant ghetto, but he didn't care. To him, it was a dedication, a religion, and a means of expression that his day job could never allow. Rodia himself said it best: "I never had a single helper. . . . Some of the people think I was crazy. . . . I wanted to do something for the United States because there are nice people in this country." And when he was seventy-four, he gave the keys to a neighbor and moved to northern California to be with family; he never saw the towers again.

The Watts Towers continue to be a source of inspiration. A park and art gallery have opened next to the work and is home to the great Watts Towers Jazz Festival every summer. It's apt that such a festival should take place under its spires, for the monument seems to be some sort of antenna reverberating with the essence of the human spirit.

And as all you rock-and-roll buffs might already know, Simon Rodia's face appears on the cover of the Beatles's *Sergeant Pepper's Lonely Hearts Club Band* album in the far upper-right corner, peeking out sideways from behind Bob Dylan's head. Rodia single-handedly built the largest and most highly individualized personal monument ever in the United States, a tribute to the dreams of the working class.

PART II

PLACES

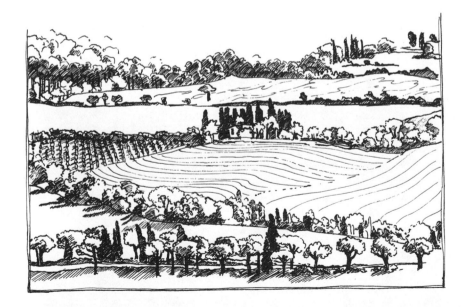

31

Apulia

Apulia is one of Italy's best-kept secrets. The heel of the Italian boot is a vast limestone plateau pointing eastward toward Albania and Greece. It is surrounded by both the Adriatic and Ionian Seas and has the most extensive coastline of any of Italy's provinces. At its top is the Promontorio del Gargano, the "spur" of the boot, a mountainous, mysterious place filled with shrines, monuments, and ancient ruins. At its southeastern tip, where the two seas merge and Italy ends, is the striking Capo di Santa Maria de Leuca. While it is not well known to foreigners, Italians travel there in large numbers to see the stunning vista from the very edge of their country.

Lello Lacerensa, the owner of the wonderful Antica Cucina restaurant in Barletta, says he thinks of Apulia as the California of southern Italy, not only because of its shape and proximity to the sea, but because, like California, it grows grains in the north, olives and grapes in its central region, and fruits and vegetables in the south. The three largest cities in the region, Bari, Brindisi, and Taranto, form a triangle, in the center of which is the fairy-tale vista of Alberobello, a little town that draws visitors from all over the world to see its famous *trulli,* round, cone-shaped white and gray houses that are absolutely unique and look like a haven for elves and gremlins.

In Apulia the connection between the food, the land, and the sea is obvious everywhere. Here the abundance of the land provides the olive oil, fruits, and vegetables that are the central elements of the Apulian table. Similarly, the abundance of the sea—its oysters, mussels, eels, crabs, and many other varieties of seafood—give that table a maritime emphasis.

Apulian food is distinctive and unusual. The region's signature pasta is called *orrechiette* (little ears), which is exactly what they look like. In Taranto, you can get a Torta Tarantina, which is essentially a pizza made with a crust of baked mashed potatoes. and Apulians are particularly fond of shellfish, especially black mussels, which appear in many dishes in a variety of guises.

Everywhere in Apulia the landscape reverberates with history and mysticism. The remarkable subterranean grottoes, interspersed throughout the region, create an intricate underground network of stalactites and stalagmites that are haunting and unforgettable. In the famous Castellana Grottoes, not far from the coastal resort of Monópoli, you feel as if you are walking along the peaks of a moon buried deep in the heart of the earth. The imposing Hohenstaufen Castle in Bari dates from the thirteenth century and looms over the city like a gigantic ship's prow turned into a fortress. In the middle of nowhere, near the small village of Gravina, you will find one of the most beautifully symmetrical buildings in all of Europe, the Castel del Monte, built by Fredrick II, where eight towers anchor its octagonal shape to the earth. This is a land filled with surprises and a source of wonderment to all who discover it. (And it's a special source of pride for the Moramarco family, whose ancestors came from this region!)

32

Bologna

Being in Bologna is like paying a visit to an Italian museum of food. That is not to say that the city itself is not remarkable; in fact, it's one of the best preserved of the old European cities. The distinctive brick architecture gives the entire city a delightful reddish hue. Bologna began its life as Felsina, a center of Etruscan culture, in the sixth century B.C. The Gauls changed the name to Bononia two centuries later. After another couple of hundred years, the Romans took over. In 1249, Bologna won its independence from Rome in the Battle of Fossalta. In spite of subsequent feudal wars, the city thrived and was eventually acquired by the papal states in the beginning of the sixteenth century. In 1860, Bologna became a part of the newly formed country of Italy.

Now, with the history out of the way, let's discuss food! Fruit markets, with mouth-watering peaches and figs, are interspersed with butcher shops, which offer the choicest meats and leanest cuts. Pasta shops boast of the best tortellini in the region and fill their windows with mounds of eye-appealing samples. Today's catch is laid out on piles of ice for all to admire at the fish market, which is next to the baker, whose crisp brown loaves have just emerged from the oven. Coffee bars, the walls lined floor to ceiling with roasted beans, are next to pastry shops, where heavenly treats make mortals pause in wonder.

Bologna is also a place where the intellect thrives. Within its city walls the first university in the world was founded in the eleventh century. With such famous alums as Dante and Petrarch, Bologna has a well-deserved reputation for being a great place to learn. Today the University of Bologna continues to feed hungry minds and draws students from all over the world. Meanwhile, the well governed city is a model for the rest of Italy, with its excellent city services and public transportation. And if you can take the time to glance up from your meal, you will see the old city center faithfully preserved in all its antiquated glory. The Piazzas Maggiore and Nettuno are pedestrian zones filled with medieval and Renaissance monuments. Nearby streets, containing buildings adorned with frescoes that haven't yet faded from view, are also well maintained. In fact, you might fancy yourself in another era entirely—if everyone wasn't talking on a cellular phone!

But let's get back to the food. Throughout Italy they say, *"Si mangia bene in Bologna."* ("You eat well in Bologna.") The city even has a sauce named after it—bolognese sauce! It's a fitting tribute to the city and its appetite for the best.

33

Florence

Florence is the city of art. The name, derived from its Roman title, "Florentia," means "destined to flourish." And flourish it has, both as home to the some of the greatest literary and artistic minds of the Renaissance and as the most popular tourist destination in all of Italy. Located in the heart of Tuscany, one of Italy's most bountiful regions, Florence blossomed like a beautiful orchid alongside the mighty Arno River.

The fifteenth and sixteenth centuries were Florence's golden age. After long periods of wars, plagues, and feuds, the city reached a state of equilibrium under the leadership of the Medici family, a clan of wealthy bankers. Their rule, while certainly not democratic, nurtured the city's intellectuals. Of all the Medicis, the greatest was Lorenzo, who ruled from 1469 to 1492. Known as "Lorenzo the Magnificent," he maintained Florence's position of power and was a great patron of the arts. One can credit him for commissioning works by, among others, Leonardo da Vinci and Sandro Botticelli and taking a young lad by the name of Michelangelo Buonarroti under his wing and providing an environment in which he could learn the art of sculpting.

Around this period, Filippo Brunelleschi was the city's chief architect, responsible not only for the striking dome of the Cathedral of Santa Maria del Fiore (simply known as the Duomo) but also the *Ospedale degli Innocenti* (the Orphanage of Florence) and the Church of Santo Spirito, among others, transforming the city into the jewel it is today. Brunelleschi's use of columns, arches, and perspective was revolutionary, and his buildings became the model other architects followed.

It was an exciting time to be alive. Advances in the arts and sciences explored the outer limits of knowledge and expanded it. Painters continued to develop the use of perspective instigated by Brunelleschi, and sculptors carved statues that captured life in motion. Books were cheap and available to all, and this was probably one of the few times in history it was actually "hip" to be smart. It was the dawning of the Rinascimento (the Renaissance), an era which began here and changed the world forever.

Fortunately, Florence's rich artistic past still exists for all to admire. A stroll through Piazza della Signoria is a who's who of great sculptors and some of their most famous works. Giambologna's *Rape of the Sabine Woman*, Cellini's bronze *Perseus*, and other notable statues are displayed in the open archways overlooking the plaza. It is here in the plaza that Michelangelo's *David* once stood before being moved to its current home in the Academy Gallery. (A replica now stands in its place.) This statue has become one of the world's best-known works of art and a symbol of Florence itself.

Next door to the plaza is the Uffizi Palace, designed and built by Giorgio Vasari. It was converted to a museum in 1581 by another Medici, Francisco I. From that point onward, the Uffizi amassed a collection of the most important art in the world, including Botticelli's *Birth of Venus,* Titian's *Venus of Urbino,* and so many more that it boggles the mind and tires the legs to see them all.

Crossing the Arno is the Ponte Vecchio, a bridge dating back to the fourteenth century. Originally, it was home to the butchers of the city, but Cosimo Medici had their shops removed and replaced them with jewelers, who have been there ever since. The stunning vista offered by the Piazzale Michelangelo, overlooking the entire city, provides a special way to absorb the magic of Florence. Another replica of *David* stands here, and during the summer months and holiday events, a fireworks display lights up the Florentine skies.

Italians are distinctly proud of Florence, its inhabitants, and the immensely important contributions the birthplace of the Renaissance has made to Western civilization.

34

Genoa

The salty port of Genoa has been an integral part of the region's commerce and transportation for hundreds of years. The ancient Ligurians were here first, using it as a gateway to the Mediterranean. The Romans walled the city in and used it as a port in their global expansion. Its most famous son is Christopher Columbus, the discoverer of the New World. But there is much more to the city that warrants its nickname of La Superba, the proud.

Genoa is the birthplace of modern trade and commerce. As the centuries passed, Genoa's importance as a trade port increased. A recently discovered contract dating from 1086 shows the extent of the Genoan trade market (reaching as far as Egypt and Morocco—a remarkably large area for the time) and outlines responsibilities of the trader and his banker. Even today it is the second largest port in the Mediterranean.

After an important victory against Venice in 1298, Genoa was at the height of its power, which lasted well into the sixteenth century. The Doria family, who ruled during much of the period, was responsible for the commissioning of some of the city's greatest buildings and palaces that line the old city squares.

Genoa has been the starting point for many important movements in Italian history. Secret meetings of the Carbonari, the incendiary group that sparked the Italian nation, began here with Guiseppe Mazzini and his followers. Later, heroic general Giuseppe Garibaldi set sail with his Mille, an all-volunteer army, to Sicily. The date of May 5, 1860, marks that historic launch, which in a matter of months led to the country's almost total unification. Genoa was also the home of the Resistance and was the first northern city to rise up against the bloody Fascist regime of Benito Mussolini, becoming independent without the aid of the Allies.

Port cities always have some great dishes, and Genoa is certainly no exception. Pesto, the wonderful sauce made from pine nuts and basil, was created here, and the deliciously thick focaccia bread that is baked here is a meal unto itself. Prawns, bass, or perch, washed down by a glass of delightful white Ligurian wine, round out a typical meal.

Today, with its comfortable climate and strong tourism and business sectors, Genoa is again becoming a booming seaside city. Looking over the harbor, as Columbus once did, you, too, can have visions of grandeur as you survey this historical town.

35

Isle of Capri

Not quite five miles long and a little over a mile wide, this little island in the Bay of Naples has been adored for centuries as a romantic, peaceful hideaway. Roman emperor Caesar Augustus loved the place, and his successor, Tiberius, was also taken by its charm. The Villa Jovis, a splendid Roman palace overlooking the entire bay, was a favorite getaway for Tiberius and many noblemen. As the centuries pass it continues to be a retreat for those who want only the best life can offer.

It's not difficult to understand why. The entire island is evocative of a fantasy land. Surrounded by reefs, hundreds of thousands of caves, and steep, jagged cliffs, it might be a place where Neptune, god of the sea, would be happy to reside. Or maybe this is how Atlantis looked before it was lost forever on the bottom of the ocean.

The *faraglioni,* large reef formations that jut over a hundred feet high from the waters around the island's perimeter, are worlds of their own. Uninhabitable by humans, these rocky mounds are home to various birds as well as the endangered blue lizard of the region. One of the formations, the Monacone, was named after the *monaca* (nun) seal that used to reside there until the last century. For its size, the island has an amazing variety of plant life. Some 850 species, including the very rare dwarf palm, flourish in its soil.

Then, of course, there is the Grotta Azurra, the alluring Blue Grotto that offers us a peek into Neptune's home. Once a Roman port, it was rediscovered in 1826 and quickly gained a reputation as one of the great natural wonders of the world. Situated just below sea level, the openings filter in light, reflecting it in such a way that the entire cavern is bathed in a beautiful blue hue, and its sandy white bottom glows silver. Today lovers of the world converge here to reaffirm their commitment to one another in the magical azure air.

Need we add that the food served on the Isle of Capri is terrific? The famous insalata caprese, a slice of tomato sprinkled with basil and olive oil and topped with a healthy slice of mozzarella, has its origins here. And you can expect the seafood to be as fresh and delicious as the pasta with which it is served.

Snorkeling, water activities, even submarine voyages, are available for all who desire them. But it is not really these things that draw people here; it is the aura of romantic magic that envelops the area. This truly is a fantasy island where lovers come to live out their fairy tales and memories they will hold for the rest of their lives.

36

The Italian Riviera

In August, when heat grips Italy's interior cities, the shopkeepers close their doors and head for the Italian Riviera. This beautiful V-shaped stretch of coastline known as Liguria is the favorite summer retreat of many Italians. From the town of Ventimiglia, which borders France, to the gorgeous vistas of La Spezia, this is Italy's summer playground. With Genoa as the anchor city at the apex of the "V," the region is divided into two sections, each with its own special attractions.

The Riviera di Ponente, located to the west of Genoa, is the hub of summer nightlife in Italy. San Remo is one of the largest and most popular of the coastal cities. With its dozens of discotheques and casinos as well as a beautiful palm tree–lined beachfront promenade, movers and shakers from all parts of Europe come here to move and shake until the wee hours of the morning. The sunny coastline has been a beacon to Europe's elite, especially to aristocrats from chilly Britain and snowy Russia, since the mid-nineteenth century. The old town, known as

La Pigna (fir cone) is a medieval labyrinth of tunnels that creates a kind of underground city and preserves a much earlier time.

On the opposite wing, heading toward Tuscany, is Riviera di Levante, quite different from the other half of the bay. Its steep and rocky cliffside views of the Mediterranean caused Charles Dickens to remark: "There is nothing in Italy more beautiful . . . than the coast road between Genoa and Spezia." Here the resort towns are a little more private, a little more low-key. The tiny town of Portofino has been transformed into a ultrahip hideaway for the wealthy. Santa Margherita and Paraggi are two other exclusive getaway spots on the coastline.

One of the most intriguing spots on the Riviera is the Cinque Terre, a unique meeting point of five tiny towns; Monterosso, Vernazza, Corniglia, Manaroloa, and Riomaggiore, all huddled around a cliffside bluff. The cities are known for some sweet white wines and still retain their charm as old fishing villages.

The Gulf of La Spezia is the last stop on the Riviera coast, and in some ways it is the best loved. It is also known as the Golfo dei Poeti, the Gulf of the Poets, for some of the greatest—Dante, Petrarch, Byron, and Shelley—found just the right words to celebrate its unique beauty and tranquil splendor. Floral-scented air, breathtaking views, splendid beaches, and cozy hideaways combine to create the endlessly fascinating Italian Rivera, a place where people go to leave the "busyness" of everyday life behind and find the poet within.

37

Lake Como

It began as a glacier at the beginning of the last ice age. When the glacier melted, the basin beneath the Grigna Mountains was filled with crystal-clear water. This is what we now know as Lake Como, one of the world's most beautiful bodies of water.

Over a hundred miles around, the lake bed has a unique shape, almost like an upside down "y." The southwest branch is called Como. There the lake's main city, Como, is located. Alessandro Volta, the Italian inventor who revolutionized the use of electricity, was born here.

Lecco, the southeast branch of the "y," carries a serene beauty all its own. It's easy to see why influential Italian author Alessandro Manzoni in 1827 set his famous historical novel *I Promessi Sposi* (*The Betrothed*) here.

Calico, the lake's northern spoke, is perhaps the most stunning of them all, with incredible views of mist-covered mountains dotted with villas. The city of Bellagio, located at the intersection of the "y," may be the ultimate spot to view the lake in all its grandeur. It is ironic that the most opulent hotel in garish Las Vegas now carries the name of this tranquil place.

Leonardo da Vinci was inspired by the natural springs at Fiume-latte. Franz Liszt was so overwhelmed by the beauty of Bellagio that he sat down and wrote his homage to Dante and Beatrice on the spot. Poets Maggi and Carlo Porta praised the incomparable Bianco Secco di Montecchia, a dry white wine from Brianza. The lake's shores have been home to many a wealthy aristocrat who decorated the surrounding areas with luxurious gardens and villas.

The summer sunsets are perhaps the most beautiful feature of Lake Como. As a lazy sun dips behind the misty mountaintops at around 10 P.M., the sky becomes a fiery red. The city lights twinkle on as the basin is slowly enveloped in darkness. The lake is calm except for tiny lighted ferries making their final runs and fishermen setting out their nets for the night. Just before the light is completely gone, the mountains are barely visible, and the fog is a pale pink. Italians surveying this heavenly scene breathe in the fresh evening air and feel truly in awe of the land they inhabit.

38

Little Italys

Wherever Italian immigrants settled in the New World, they brought with them a rich heritage that they preserved in enclaves where they lived close to one another in America's major cities: New York, Baltimore, Boston, Chicago, San Francisco, Los Angeles, even San Diego. Each of these cities, and many more, has its own "Little Italy," an island of beautifully preserved and maintained Italian culture where the food, language, and traditions of Italy thrive and blossom.

Little Italy in New York is the oldest and most famous of these. Located in the southeastern part of Manhattan Island, the neighborhood is home to over forty of New York's best Italian restaurants and is a visitor's mecca for travelers from all over the world. The world-famous Feast of San Gennaro, a tribute to the patron saint of Naples, attracts some three million visitors each September who revel in the ten-day celebration of food, music, dancing, and other expressions of Italian-American culture. Boston's Little Italy is proud to have a statue of American hero Paul Revere in its midst, a symbol of freedom in the New World. Chicago's Little Italy boasts friendly restaurants and is home to the deep-dish pizza that is referred to simply as "Chicago style."

On the opposite coast, San Francisco's North Beach district, which bills itself as "San Francisco's Little Italy and Home of the Beat Generation," is famous for its many restaurants and landmarks associated with its early Italian settlers. North Beach is also home to the Italian-American Athletic Club, which sponsors one of the oldest continuing footraces in America, the Statuto Race, which has been held without fail on the first Sunday in June since 1918.

Just north of San Diego's downtown area is India Street, a stretch, several blocks long, of Italian groceries, restaurants, pastry shops, and cafes. India Street is home to an annual Columbus Day festival during which the streets come alive with the sounds, smells, and colors of Italy.

Back east, Baltimore's Little Italy, a neighborhood located adjacent to Baltimore's famous Inner Harbor, has been treating visitors to Italian culinary delicacies for years. Settled in the early part of the twentieth century, the neighborhood around Albemarle, Fawn, and High Street is still predominantly Italian. Many of the unique brownstones with characteristic front "stoops" have been in the same family for generations.

Each of these neighborhoods is a living gallery of Italian-American culture. They remind us how our immigrant ancestors needed to stick together to survive and how firm they were in their determination to preserve the culture of their homeland. Whenever you're in an American city and don't know where to find a good restaurant, it's a safe bet that in Little Italy you'll have plenty of good choices. After all, as Neil Simon said, "There are two laws in the universe: The law of gravity and everyone loves Italian food."

39

Milan

Milan is Italy at its most modern. From its position near the top of the boot, Milan leads, and the rest of the world follows. After World War I, Milan became the center of the garment industry, with its fabulous fabric and leather products. In the fifties and sixties it began to sucessfully market the Italian look around the globe. Since then, it has become the epicenter of the fashion world.

Its most famous fashion designer is, of course, Giorgio Armani, who began as a buyer for menswear here in the 1950s. But Milan continues to be in the forefront of fashion, with designers and shows that make international news.

Milan is also a leader in sports and entertainment. La Scala, the most famous opera house in the world, is here. Since its opening in 1778, it has garnered a reputation for excellence in acoustics. For soccer fans, Milan is home to two of the world's greatest teams, A. C. Milan and Internazionale, referred to as Inter by the locals.

To say Milan is modern or industrial may imply that it is not beautiful, which is simply not true. At the city's center stands one of the great architectural wonders of the world, the Duomo, in Piazza del Duomo. Over five hundred years in the making, the huge, ornate Gothic cathedral is adorned with more than three thousand statues. Perego's *Madonnina*, residing at the cathedral's highest point since 1744, has become the city's emblem. The Duomo sits at the center of Milanese life, a spiritual assertion in the midst of the world of commerce and fashion.

Another striking architectural monument in Milan is the imposing Castello Sforzesco. It is a bastion of the Sforza clan, who ruled Milan from 1450 to 1535. The last of the lineage of the Sforza family, Lodovico Sforza, was a great patron of the arts. It is to his credit that Leonardo da Vinci's *Last Supper* (1498) was painted at the monastery in Santa Maria Delle Grazie, for he frequently commissioned artists and architects to beautify Milan's churches. The Parco Sempione and the Giardini Pubblici are two of the city's largest parks and are covered with grass, filled with flowers, and shaded with tall trees.

Italians can be proud of Milan and its contribution to twentieth-century culture. Its factories provide food and supplies for many regions. It is a city that is always on the cutting edge. Its innovative tendencies will propel Italian culture into the next century with dignity.

40

Naples

"Vedi Napoli e poi muori" ("See Naples and then die.") Although this saying is meant to capture the power and beauty of this historic southern city, it could also be interpreted literally: You could step off the curb and be hit by an erratic Neapolitan driver. Naples, more than any other Italian city, seems to crackle with nonstop motion and energy.

The residents of Naples hold their city close to the heart. Why? Sloping down from Campi Flegrei to the Bay of Naples and ending at the foot of the ominous, dormant volcano Mount Vesuvius, it offers a vista of the Mediterranean that is sublime.

The Neapolitan passion for their town extends back to its beginnings as a Greek settlement named Neapolis (New City) by its founders, who were mesmerized by the locale. In the fourteenth century "Good King" Robert of Anjou opened the city's ports to artists and poets of the Continent, and many, including Boccaccio, Petrarch, and Giotto, called this town their home. Architects Lorenzo Bernini and Luigi Vanvitelli lived here, as well as seminal opera singer Enrico Caruso.

But there is something else here about the city that can't quite be put into words. A mystical quality transfixes the whole place. Giuseppe Sanmartino's *Veiled Christ,* on display in the Cappella Sansevero, still baffles experts, who have yet to figure out how he sculpted this seemingly translucent veil. Nearby, in the Church of San Domenico, a painting of the crucifixion is purported to have spoken to Saint Thomas Aquinas. Every year during the Festival of San Gennaro, the patron saint of Naples, thousands gather to see if the ancient vials of the saint's blood will liquefy once again. If it does, as the natives say it has regularly since A.D. 305, the city will be saved from disaster. When the miracle failed in 1941, Mount Vesuvius erupted.

Naples is also home to many wonderful and underrated museums, including the Capo di Monte, with its impressive collection of Italian art. And let it not be forgotten that Naples is the home of the pizza. The Tavern of Cerriglio, in the seventeenth century, was the first place in the world to sell a tomato-based mozzarella pizza.

In the past few years, Naples has made an impressive effort to clean up its streets and restore many of its historic buildings, revitalizing pride in this wonderful city. So take a bite of your favorite slice, think of Old Napoli, and let all her sins be forgiven.

41

Pompeii

When Mount Vesuvius erupted on August 24, A.D. 79, the Roman town of Pompeii was bombarded with *lapilli,* hot fragments of pumice, and two thousand of its twenty thousand inhabitants perished. The town was covered with ash and rock for centuries, practically forgotten to the world.

In 1594 architect Domenico Fontana uncovered a section of the city while building a canal. But it wasn't until 1860, under the guidance of Giuseppe Fiorelli, that much of the excavation got under way. What he uncovered was startling.

The ruins of Pompeii provide some of the best-preserved evidence of the Roman lifestyle. Rather than being plundered and rebuilt like many other cities, its fate under Vesuvius was quick. The lava and ash preserved the town in action, in the middle of the day, at the height of the Roman Empire. Its ruins are like a snapshot of another civilization.

Pompeii had been a bustling commercial city, its streets crowded with vendors and citizens. It possessed a temple dedicated to Apollo, where people paid tribute to the gods of music, poetry, prophecy, and medicine; a forum, which was in the center of town; theaters; and various shops and houses. You can still see intricate mosaics that lined the floors as well as some beautiful paintings. In the former mansions of the rich, there's evidence of running water for baths and toilets, and grooves in the roadways show the paths the chariots took. One can also see graffiti of schoolchildren, announcements of gladiatorial contests, coins and pens, and even fossilized remnants of food cooked that fateful day the sky turned black with soot and the streets became rivers of molten lava.

But there's more. Fiorelli, while painstakingly excavating the ruins from the ash, saw that the actual bodies of citizens of Pompeii were imprinted in the fine layer of silt. He developed a revolutionary technique to make plaster casts of these impressions, and the result is horrific, tragic, and beautiful all at once. Real beings, in the midst of a terrible act of nature, stand frozen at the moment of their demise. A man lies face down, his hand covering his eyes; a dog twists its body in agony. These statues have such an impact on the viewer because you know they were once living, breathing entities.

Pompeii was a city that one moment was basking in the glory of the Roman Empire and the next consumed by the lava of Vesuivus. Triumph and tragedy exist side by side; that disaster has allowed our civilization to glimpse its splendors.

42

Ravenna

Ravenna is the city of mosaics. Its amazing collection of murals, created using millions of tiny pieces of colored marble and stone, are remnants from the early Christian and Byzantine eras.

The city's history is unique. It became the capital of the western Roman Empire in A.D. 402, when Emperor Honorius decided the surrounding swamps made it easier to defend than Rome. Later, it became the capital of Theodoric the Great's rule as king of the Ostrogoths in Italy. In A.D. 540, Ravenna became the seat of the eastern Roman Empire, when Emperor Justinian's army marched in from Byzantium.

All through this period the art of the mosaic thrived. Inspired by the Greeks and Romans, artisans created intricate works using marble and other material. Each piece of *tessera* (marble, glass, or tile) was handpicked, cut, and set in place one by one. By the time of the Byzantines, the art form had reached its zenith, and the walls and churches of Ravenna are the surviving testament to this delicate art.

The Basilica di San Vitale is one of the great examples of this handiwork, showing scenes from the Old Testament as well as Emperor Justinian and Empress Theodora within its walls. The juxtaposition of Greek style, Christian symbolism, and Byzantine splendor give the reliefs a unique beauty. As candlelight dances against the golden surface, one has to look twice to appreciate not only the majesty of the art but also the meticulousness of the craft that created it.

The art of the mosaic still thrives here. The tradition, which has been handed down through the ages, continues to dazzle visitors, with new artisans displaying their works, making Ravenna the unquestioned mosaic capital of the West.

Dante loved this city. After being banished from Florence in 1302, he found sanctuary in Ravenna. Here he wrote the bulk of his *Divine Comedy,* a trilogy of poems on Heaven, Hell, and Purgatory that changed literature forever. (See chapter 52.) He was laid to rest here in 1321, the area around his tomb marked as a *zona di silenzio* in honor of this great man.

Ravenna is beautiful, and its citizens have made important contributions to art, politics, and literature. Like a precious stone, it has a special place in the mosaic of Italian pride.

43

Rome

Rome is the mother of all cities. Currently the capital of Italy, Rome was for centuries the center of the known Western world. Legend has it that two brothers, Romulus and Remus, who were cast upon the Tiber River and raised by a she-wolf, founded the city. The image of the two children suckling on the beast has been the city's symbol since the earliest Roman days.

While the history of the area reaches even further back to the Etruscans, April 21, 753 B.C., is regarded by Romans as the founding date; on this day Romulus killed Remus and took control of the city. The legend goes on to say that Romulus disappeared one day in a puff of smoke, sent back to the gods, whence he came.

Although the story is just an ancient folktale, it's easy to see why it has been told for centuries. Rome feels like a mythical place. Surrounded by seven hills, the city has been toppled and rebuilt many times, each regime erecting its own monuments on top of, and next to, the remains of the previous. The result is a staggering hodgepodge of history. Roman arches stand adjacent (and inside) medieval and Renaissance buildings. Ancient Egyptian obelisks decorate piazzas. Deep below the city are catacombs housing remnants of the Christian martyrs who were killed for sport in the Colosseum. An eighteenth-century synagogue resides in the sixteenth-century Jewish ghetto, near a bridge dating from 62 B.C. Today roadways swirl around these sites, cars honking and people yelling; modern Romans, in their "chariots," taking command of their streets. The Colosseum is but a majestic ruin, a tourist

hot spot and home to about a million cats that are protected by the state like an endangered species. A popular saying here is *"Roma, non basta una vita!"* ("For Rome, a life is not enough!") to truly enjoy the splendors of a city almost three thousand years old.

Rome still harnesses its ancient power. This is where Augustus Caesar commanded ships and troops throughout Europe, Africa, and the East, creating the largest empire in the world. This is where Brutus betrayed Julius Caesar and Shakespeare has Marc Antony making his famous "Friends, Romans, Countrymen," speech. This is where the early Christians were thrown to the lions and where the Emperor Constantine finally recognized Christianity in A.D. 313. This is the empire that Spartacus revolted against. This is where Nero fiddled while the city burned. This is where all roads lead. This is where we do as the Romans do. This is it.

On September 20, 1870, Rome became the capital of a united Italy and the home to Italian government ever since. Italy's governments have been famous for their instability, but the late 1990s saw an unprecedented amount of reform as the government prepared for European economic unification in 2002. Italians take pride in the ancient and modern cities of Rome as a continuing leader of world trends, a tradition as old as the Roman city walls that encircle it.

44

Sardinia

Geologically, Sardinia is the oldest region in the entire country of Italy, so we might say that Italian pride was born here. Six hundred million years ago this rock surfaced from the depths of the sea, before most of continental Europe. Consequently, much of the island has a natural, prehistoric beauty. Jagged granite masses, thick black bushes, and dense pine forests recall a time long before humans set foot on this soil.

This natural beauty, as well as its pristine beaches, continue to make Sardinia an excellent vacation spot. The Costa Smeralda (Emerald Coast) of the northwest, the luxurious resorts of Porto Cervo, and beaches such as Baia Sardinia and Porto Quato all contain sun, sand, and sea in their purest forms.

And it is rich in history. The tiny islet of Caprera, off the northwest tip, is where famed Italian general Garibaldi spent his last days after successfully uniting Italy under one king. His home is now a museum.

The island's capital, Cagliari, is also an enchanting place, with its own exquisite beaches, medieval artifacts, and even pink flamingos. It is believed to have been founded by the Phoenicians around 1000 B.C.

If you can tear yourself away from its shores, you will see other things that make the island truly special. Ancient arrowheads are found here in abundance, and the *nuraghi,* round stone fortresses dating back to 1500 B.C., are evidence of a lost civilization that once ruled the isle.

Deep in the heart of Sardinia is the Barbagia region, where time stands still. Named after the Roman word for barbarian, this mountainous area has been hidden away for centuries. Its people, however, are anything but barbaric. Extremely friendly, they are proud of their ancient traditions. Shepherds still live in stone huts, and many of the women still don the traditional veiled garb of their ancestors.

Conversely, in the south, the city of Oristano offers a look into the beginnings of feminism. Eleonora d'Arborera, strongly opposed to its Spanish sovreignity, ruled the city in the fourteenth century. She is responsible for drawing up the Carta de Logu, a series of laws that would eventually govern the island. The document is one of the few surviving recordings of the ancient Sardinian language. Oristano has had several women leaders since then, and the Sardinian Woman's Cooperative of Sheep-Breeders is a thriving agricultural and tourist enterprise. It's an entirely different Italy than its boot-shaped relative— rugged, rural, and unspoiled.

45

Sicily

The warm, fertile climate of Italy's largest island is a wonder to experience. Miles of beaches, active volcanoes, and a distinct southern hospitality add cadence and variety to the natural poetry of the land itself.

Located in the middle of the Mediterranean, it is positioned like a soccer ball that the boot-shaped continent is kicking. The metaphor is somewhat apt, for Sicily has had its share of hard knocks, The Sicanis, Elymians, and Siculians were some of the island's first inhabitants. The Greeks landed here in the eighth century B.C., discovering and developing a new part of their empire. Then came the Romans, Byzantines, Arabs, Normans, Swabians, Angevins, and Bourbons, each having their era of dominance over Sicily. General Garibaldi landed on its shores with his army, the Mille, beginning his sweep of Italy that united the country. During the final phase of World War II, the Allies took Sicily's beaches back from the Fascists, which helped end Mussolini's regime.

The Sicilian soil has become incredibly fertile from the combination of sun and moisture that saturates the land. The succulent blood oranges, lemons, and tomatoes that thrive here revitalize the soul and connect the eater with ancestors who must have enjoyed these same types of fruits from the same sacred earth. The very name "blood oranges" not only describes the color of this distinctly Sicilian fruit; it also suggests the vitality of the earth here as well as the passion of its people.

Palermo is Sicily's capital, and its architectural style shows the influence of both East and West. Its Duomo is an eclectic combination of many styles—Gothic, Baroque, Moroccan, and Classical. With its narrow streets and open-air markets, there is a sense of a bustling communal lifestyle that fills the air. While the city has suffered the aforementioned hard knocks, it is currently experiencing a revitalization as it cleanses itself of its Mafia past and rebuilds its infrastructure.

Volcanoes are alive and well in Sicily, and Mount Etna is the most famous. The largest volcano in Europe, it is still quite active. The blackened slopes of the mountain are continually highlighted with red-hot pools of lava, which regularly are emitted from its numerous craters. Its "minor" eruptions provide a majestic fireworks show, put on by nature herself.

Almost everywhere you go, you can get some of the freshest and sweetest gelato in Italy, dine on swordfish and other fruits of the sea, and be treated with a kindness and respect that is trademark in the region.

46

Siena

Siena is a city from another time. Nestled in the heart of Tuscany among three hills, Siena's atmosphere and traditions have remained untouched since medieval days. No one is quite sure when it arose. Legend has it that it was founded by the son of Remus, one of the twins who founded Rome. It was most certainly a Roman military outpost named Sena Julia in 1 B.C. and from there developed into a city.

During the thirteenth century, the town reached its peak as a sovereign power. Ruled by the Council of Nine, comprised of people from the middle class, Siena was an autonomous and fiercely independent city-state. Many of its most beautiful buildings were erected during this time in wonderful Gothic style.

Today the city is most famous for Il Palio. A horse race, a parade, a neighborhood rivalry, a feast, and a party all in one, it is one of the oldest and most popular festivals in all of Italy. Every July 2 the city is filled with people and charged with electricity as Il Palio begins.

Dressed in medieval costume, each of the seventeen *contrade* (neighborhoods) parade through the street, proudly waving their group's flag. These include the Dragon, the She-Wolf, the Giraffe, and even the Hedgehog. Each contrade draws a lot to see which horse it will ride and where it will be in the starting line. The contrade in the last position decides when the race will start, and it is his duty to distract and mislead the others so that he has a better chance of winning. Sometimes it takes up to two hours after the drawing for the race to actually start, but when it does—wham!—seventeen medieval jockeys ride bareback through the beautiful Piazza del Campo, whipping the horses and each other in this chaotic, anything-goes race. A mere seventy-five seconds later, it's all over, and the winning contrade receives a banner that it proudly hangs in its neighborhood.

Feasts galore follow, and the streets are filled with emotion as spectators, winners, and losers all converge, venting their feelings after this climactic event. For the defeated contrade, it's not to worry: they'll have another chance on August 16, when the second Palio of the year is celebrated.

The rivalries between the various factions also serve to bring them closer together, for they all know they are part of a culture and event that have existed for a very long time. The victories are sweet and the defeats bitter, but it's all just a fact of life here in Siena, where tradition is part of the very air one breathes.

47

Tuscany

If Florence is the heart of the Renaissance, Tuscany, the province in which Florence is situated, is its body and soul. Culturally, historically, economically, and gastronomically, this is one of the richest parts of Italy. This region, running along the "upper thigh" of the boot on the Mediterranean coastline, contains many of the country's most important cities and was home to its most influential personalities.

Because the area gave birth to a new kind of art and literature which influenced the rest of the Continent and the world, it is here that *la lingua italiana* (see chapter 13) is spoken in its purest form. The finest olive oil and superior wines practically gush from its soil. Tuscan food is an art form in itself, with bread and oil staple ingredients of almost every course. The famous twice-boiled soup, ribollita, spills from the ladles of restaurants everywhere, and the bistecca alla fiorentina, a grilled steak with a bit of Tuscan olive-oil goodness, fills the nostrils with its hearty aroma and satisfies the taste buds with its unmistakable flavor. Wild game and boar constitute more exotic elements of the Tuscan palate, making every meal a culinary *paradiso,* especially if washed down with a brimming glass of Chianti wine.

And then there are the cities, each with its own uniquely beautiful personality. There's Lucca, a tiny walled town that was one of the first of the independent city-states, which flourished with the silk trade. And charming Carrara, whose marble was handpicked from the quarries by Michelangelo for many of his masterpieces. In the east, there's Arezzo, with its famous fresco cycle by Piero della Francesca and renowned antique fairs, and in the hills there are the towers that form the medieval skyline of San Gimignano.

The isle of Elba, where Napoleon was exiled, floats majestically off the coastline and its environment is a haven for nature lovers. The Garfagnana offers excellent trails for hiking and horseback riding around the Serchio River. And Maremma, with its cowboys riding *maremmano* horses, herding bulls in fields of wheat, is Italy's wild west.

Together, these elements produce a fabled area whose people and places have changed the world. The Tuscan countryside is a place to wander, to dawdle, to savor the slowness of the day and the beauty of nature's abundance. We heartily agree with Frances Mayes, author of the *Under the Tuscan Sun:* "My idea of heaven," she writes, "is to drive the gravel roads of . . . Tuscany, very pleasantly lost."

48

Vatican City

The center of the Roman Catholic world, Vatican City is where *il papa*, the pope, and the Sacred College of Cardinals reside and direct the doctrines of the church. Every Wednesday, the pope gives an audience to hundreds of followers. On holy days, he speaks in Saint Peter's Square, delivering his message to a crowd gathered in the plaza and the world.

The history of the area goes back to the earliest days of Christianity. Saint Peter, a disciple of Jesus and the first pope, was buried here in A.D. 67. In 315, the emperor Constantine began construction of a church to commemorate the saint. Since 1377, the magnificent basilica built in his honor has been the seat of the papacy.

Located within Rome, the Vatican is a self-governing city within a city. The Lateran Treaty of 1929 awarded the pope sole sovereignty of Vatican City. The Swiss Guards, who protect the pope and cardinals, wear uniforms that were most likely designed by Michelangelo.

Even for people of other faiths, the Vatican is still a marvel to behold. Saint Peter's Basilica, took over 150 years to complete and contains masterpieces by some of the world's greatest artists, including Raphael, Donato Bramante, Carlo Maderno, and of course, Michelangelo, who, at seventy-two, was the primary architect of the church's dome and painter of the stunning ceiling of the Sistine Chapel, an amazing rendering of the Creation and the Last Judgment. The ceiling was painstakingly restored in the 1990s and can now once again be viewed in all its grandeur.

The piazza in front of the church, designed by Bernini, is also an architectural masterpiece. Two semicircles of colonnades, dotted with statues of saints, surround the entrance. In the center stands an Egyptian obelisk brought to Rome by the emperor Caligula and placed in the center of the square by Pope Sixtus V.

Inside the church itself one can see Michelangelo's *Pietà* and Arnolfo di Cambio's *St. Peter,* whose foot has been rubbed smooth by the hands of the devoted. The pope's high altar stands over Peter's grave, a living emblem of Christ's famous words, "Thou art Peter, and upon this rock I will build my church."

One of the most emotional events in a Catholic's life occurs when he or she can visit this city and feel the presence and power of the Holy Spirit. The Vatican, with its message of peace and hope for all, continues to be a source of inspiration to millions of followers around the world.

49

Venice

Quite simply, there is no place on earth like Venice. It is a city built upon the sea. One hundred eighteen tiny islets, developed through centuries of human innovation, constitute this immortal city. It was founded in the fifth and sixth centuries when a group of settlers forged their own city in the lagoon to escape from barbarian invasions. Over eleven hundred years later, the majestic city still floats, as beautiful as ever.

Venice is, of course, a port. The market at the Rialto Bridge has long been the place for merchants from around the globe to sell their wares. The city has been a world leader in the production of lace since A.D. 1100. And Murano glass, hand blown and using the same tools in the same ovens for centuries, has known no equal for its perfection and beauty.

Like a rose, Venice bloomed into a place of unsurpassed beauty. Piazza San Marco, the city center, is a harmonious convergence of earth, art, and sea. The Basilica San Marco, with its extraordinary domes and mosaics; the majestic Clock Tower, with its bronze Moors coming to life via an ancient system of gears ringing the bell situated between them with hammers every hour; and the Gothic majesty of the Doges Palace, which housed a succession of magistrates who enjoyed uninterrupted leadership of the city and its canals for more than a millennium, all overlook the Grand Canal, the city's main waterway. For many years, the Doge would drop a ring into the ocean, symbolizing the marriage of Venice to its watery surroundings.

Also, like a rose, Venice is the symbol of romance. One of the main forms of transportation, the gondola, has become the scene of many a marriage proposal and subsequent honeymoon. These long, flat boats travel silently through the watery streets and under the bridges, giving lovers (and others) a perfect view of the walkways and buildings that dot the islets.

The labyrinth of tiny streets that crisscross Venice are a treasure trove of interesting sights. One merely needs to step out of the bustle of the main areas to discover hidden monuments and buildings. Its stillness earned it the nickname La Serenissima, or the Most Serene. The winged lion, perched atop a pedestal in Piazza San Marco, is its symbol.

Venice is a living dream. Walking its streets or riding in its gondolas, sitting in the plaza, or admiring its distinctive architecture and Renaissance art, one can see that its contribution to Italian pride is everywhere apparent. It is truly one of a kind.

50

Verona

Ahh, "fair Verona," as one of Shakespeare's characters once called it. Dressed in the rose-colored marble that is indigenous to the region, the city and its buildings glow like the flushed cheeks of young lovers. That's quite appropriate, for it is the setting of one of the Bard's most famous and romantic plays, *Romeo and Juliet*.

Of course, those star-crossed lovers never actually existed, but within this township they are treated as historical figures. One can gaze at Juliet's balcony, see where Romeo lived, and visit the former monastery that houses Juliet's "tomb." Its part of the blend of fantasy and reality that gives Verona its romantic charm. The Cappello and Montecchi families, upon whom Shakespeare based his warring Montague and Capulet factions, did exist, but it is doubtful they were much in conflict. Still, romance is always in the air here as millions come every year to vicariously live out Shakespeare's poetic tragedy.

Verona is a small town, known as Piccola Roma, Little Rome,

because it was an important city during the the Roman era. Nowadays it is one of the most peaceful and prosperous cities in all of Italy, one whose majestic past is on display for all to see.

The Piazza Brà is a popular city center where Veronese eat, drink, and gather along the *liston,* a collection of cafes around its perimeter. Boiled meats and fresh vegetables are common dishes, and the wines of choice are the dry white Soave or the crimson Valpolicella. Over the Piazza looms the majestic Roman Arena, from the first century A.D., which is still in use as an opera house and theater. On warm summer evenings, a stroll around the Adige River, which encircles the city, is a perfect way to cap a wonderful day.

The city's most beautiful church, the Basilica di San Zeno Maggiore, is named after Verona's patron saint. One of his most famous miracles involved rescuing a man from an attack of wild oxen by making the sign of the cross, an event commemorated in a painting by Nicolas Pisano inside the church.

The city is also the backdrop of another of Shakespeare's plays, aptly entitled *The Two Gentlemen of Verona,* one of his earliest, liveliest comedies. No doubt Shakespeare chose the city as his setting because the Veronese people are indeed always lively and the streets echo with laughter. Verona is the perfect place for poets, lovers, and dreamers.

51

Via Appia

Should Italians be proud they invented the first freeway? Of course! This miracle of transportation was responsible for the evolution of modern society. And the Romans, who developed (and conquered) much of the Western world, were definitely on the ball when it came to getting around.

Known in its day as Regina Viarum (Queen of the Roads), it was begun by Appius Claudius Caecus in 312 B.C. By around 190 B.C., it had stretched across the peninsula to connect with Brindisi in the region of Apulia. It was the only connection to Greece and the empires beyond. Hundreds of tombs from twenty generations of Roman noblility line miles of the roadside, where it was considered an honor to be buried.

Along the first part of the road, Via Porta San Sebastiano, is what could be called one of the first fitness clubs. The baths of Caracalla could handle over fifteen hundred bathers. It contained gymnasiums, gardens, and magnificent rooms for hot, warm, or cold baths.

The stretch of the road from Rome to Terracina is something of a scientific wonder because it is almost perfectly straight. It is along this road that a spot has been immortalized as Quo Vadis, where the disciple Peter saw a vision of Christ, which made him return to Rome for martyrdom.

The road was a burial place for not only the rich. Alongside and underneath the stretch of roadways is the amazingly complex series of tombs known as the Catacombs, the burial ground for hundreds of early Christians. From the first to the fourth centuries, when Christianity was outlawed by the Romans, the devoted literally had to take their religion underground, and these labyrinthine passages became both their hideout and their final resting places.

The Via Appia is a stretch of roadway that encapsulates almost the entire history of the Western Hemisphere, a crossroads where Caesar and Christ met. Its precision and grandeur literally paved the way for trade and transportation, and its underground tunnels literally forged a new religion. The ruins of the roadway stand as a reminder of the rich and the poor, the privileged and the punished, who built the foundations of our Italian heritage on this sacred ground.

PART III

PEOPLE

52

Dante Alighieri

Dante is so famous that we refer to him only by his first name. When he decided to write *The Divine Comedy,* his masterpiece, in the language spoken in Florence rather than in Latin, the literary language of his day, he succeeded in establishing the Tuscan dialect as "official" Italian for centuries to come. Born in Florence in 1265, he heralded the dawning of that great rebirth of classical humanism that led to the Renaissance. Because *The Divine Comedy* was written as an allegory—that is, a literary work with meanings beyond the literal—it has occasioned more critical commentary and exegeses than any book in Western civilization other than the Bible.

The Divine Comedy (Dante called it the *Commedia;* the adjective "Divine" was added by critics in the sixteenth century) is the story of a pilgrim's journey through Hell, Purgatory, and Paradise, and it is from this monumental work that we get our modern conception of these otherworldly places. The pilgrim is guided by the great Latin poet Virgil, whose *Aeneid* is Dante's literary model. The epic also immortalizes Dante's extraordinary love for Beatrice, a woman he first met as a child. Dante carried Beatrice in his soul for his entire life, although both he and she married others; she died in 1290, some thirty-one years before he did (in 1321). In *The Divine Comedy*, he must traverse the depths of human suffering and depravity and the middle ground of human desire and indecision before encountering her again in the bright light of Paradise, the epitome of human harmony and possibility.

The poetry of *The Divine Comedy* is unparalleled in world literature. Translators have particular difficulty with the verse form—a highly disciplined *terza rima,* or interlocking, rhymed three-line stanzas. Some translators abandon any attempt to imitate the form of the poem; others merely approximate it. From the opening lines of the *Inferno* (the journey through Hell) the reader finds himself identifying with the narrator, who has lost his way in life and is searching for the right path:

> Midway on our life's journey, I found myself
> In dark woods, the right road lost.

Dante's Hell is both real and a state of mind, and Dante's echoing phrase tells us exactly what it feels like:

> Abandon all hope, you who enter here.

53

Christopher Columbus

Christopher Columbus's reputation has waxed and waned over the years, depending on the politics of the day and the perspective from which his accomplishments are viewed. Columbus was not a saintly man. In fact, he was specifically denied beatification by the Catholic church because he lived with an unmarried woman, had a child out of wedlock, and kidnapped and enslaved hundreds of indigenous peoples that he offered for sale in Europe. And yet there is surely no other explorer in history who has had as profound an impact on the shape and direction of the modern world. Columbus ventured beyond the Pillars of Hercules, the mythological name given to the rock formations flanking the Straits of Gibraltar that marked, in his time, the end of the known world. To sail beyond that point was to venture into the unknown.

Born in 1451 in the port city of Genoa, Columbus had several careers—as a weaver, a merchant seaman, and a mapmaker—before embarking on the voyage that was to assure his place in history. He was not the only mariner who believed that the earth was shaped like a sphere and that if you sailed far enough in a westerly direction you would land somewhere in Asia. But what differentiated Columbus from the others who believed this was his fortitude and persistence. For nearly a decade he continually attempted to persuade the monarchs of Portugal and Spain to support an expedition into the open ocean beyond the Pillars of Hercules. Again and again he was told that such a voyage was impractical and prohibitive financially. At last, in 1492 he convinced King Ferdinand and Queen Isabella of Spain to sponsor his venture, and the rest, as they say, is history. On October 12, the day we now celebrate as Columbus Day, he landed in the Bahamas on the island of San Salvador, later one of the British West Indies. Upon his return to Spain, he was declared the "Admiral of the Open Sea" and almost immediately began preparations for the second voyage.

In all, Columbus made four voyages across the Atlantic, each time discovering new terrain and immensely expanding our knowledge and understanding of the planet. Ironically, he died (in 1506) never knowing that the lands he encountered were not part of Asia at all but a whole new world. Although he remains a controversial figure to this day, Italians are justifiably proud of the persistence and vision of the Genoese sailor with a dream who truly transformed the world.

54

Joe DiMaggio

On the day of Joe DiMaggio's funeral (March 11, 1999), a barrista at the famous Cafe Roma coffee shop in San Francisco's Italian neighborhood of North Beach told a reporter: "*Oggi parlo Italiano* for Joe!"—"Today I will speak Italian for Joe." It was his way of demonstrating his pride in the life as well as the heroic stature of Joltin' Joe DiMaggio, the "Yankee Clipper," in American culture.

DiMaggio, was a hero's hero—a quiet, unassuming man who still holds the record for hitting safely in 56 consecutive games. Born to an Italian-American family in Martinez, California, DiMaggio played for the New York Yankees from 1936 until his retirement in 1951. To play for one team for one's entire athletic career is virtually unheard of today, but DiMaggio was a New York Yankee through and through. His number, 5, was long ago retired at Yankee Stadium, where a monument to his unequaled contribution to the team stands behind the center field wall.

DiMaggio is still regarded as one of the best outfielders in baseball history. He played in ten World Series, and was the American League's Most Valuable Player in 1939, 1941, and 1947. In 1948, in the twilight of his career, he led the league with 39 home runs and 155 runs batted in. In 1955, DiMaggio was inducted into the Major League Baseball Hall of Fame in Cooperstown, New York.

DiMaggio further added to his status as an American icon when he married Marilyn Monroe in 1954. Although the marriage lasted only several months, DiMaggio remained deeply devoted to Marilyn. Rumour had it that they were planning to be remarried shortly before her death in 1962. For over twenty years DiMaggio saw to it that flowers were delivered weekly to her crypt, for he had promised Marilyn he would do this when she told him of William Powell's pledge to the dying Jean Harlow.

In 1986, DiMaggio received the Ellis Island Medal of Honor for his baseball achievements as well as for being a worthy role model for America's youth. He was once asked by an interviewer why he thought his popularity had endured so long. With characteristic humility he replied: "I wish I could tell you what the answer is. I've tried to answer that question many times. I'm just Joe. I'm the same kid as when I played with the San Francisco Seals."

America needs more heroes like Joe DiMaggio, an immigrant's son who was a big leaguer in all aspects of his life.

55

Federico Fellini

In 1993, the American Academy of Motion Picture Arts and Sciences honored Federico Fellini with its prestigious Lifetime Achievement Award, a tribute that came none too soon, since Fellini died in October of that same year at the age of seventy-three. In his speech accepting the award, Fellini dedicated it to his wife of fifty years, Giulietta Masina, who acted in many of his films and was the inspiration for much of his work. His marvelous *Juliet of the Spirits* (1965) is a tribute to her and to the strength and fortitude of women everywhere. His career in films covered nearly a half century, during which time he directed several of the most memorable and distinctive films ever made, including *La Strada* (1954), *La Dolce Vita* (1960), *8½* (1963), *Fellini Satyricon* (1969), and *Amarcord* (1974).

The first film to gain him international recognition was *La Strada*, which won the Academy Award for Best Foreign Film in 1954. In it, one can already see the trademark elements that were to characterize his later work and lead to the creation of the awkward adjective "Felliniesque," meaning a kind of playful surrealism that is grounded in the solid reality of everyday Italian life. First of all, it is about a circus, a recurring Fellini metaphor for life itself in its amazing variety and unpredictability. It is filled with parades, processions, and other metaphors for the journey through life that mark almost all of his films.

In the early 1960s, Fellini directed two films back-to-back that assured him a place in cinema history and solidified his reputation as a great original. *La Dolce Vita* chronicled the "sweet life" of the "beautiful people" in upper-middle-class Italian society of the day, a social class that he saw immersed in decadence and hedonism. The opening shot of the film is classic Fellini, capturing in a single image the contradictions of contemporary Italy. In it, a helicopter transports a statue of Christ over the rooftops of Rome, where women are sunbathing in bikinis—the life of the spirit has been usurped by the life of the body and material comfort. The film was unsparing in its satirical critique of all aspects of Italian society. As a result, the film was widely condemned in Italy by both the church and the government at the same time that its frank portrayal of an unbridled sexuality made it a box-office hit throughout the world.

His next film, *8½* (so called because Fellini had directed seven previous films and part of one other), has been called by Leonard Maltin "one of the most intensely personal statements ever made on celluloid."

It is about an internationally acclaimed director struggling to decide what film to make next. Once again, it is filled with riveting images, like the Roman traffic jam that opens the film, which becomes a symbol for modern man trapped in his own urban technological nightmare.

Upon Fellini's death, Stanley Kauffman, the distinguished film critic of the *New Republic,* spoke for so many of Fellini's admirers when he wrote: "During his lifetime, many fine filmmakers blessed us with their art, but he was the only one who made us feel that each of his films, whatever its merits, was a present from a friend."

56

Dario Fo and Franca Rame

In 1997, when Dario Fo won the world's most prestigious literary award, the Nobel Prize in literature, few Americans had ever heard of him. Who was this obscure Italian playwright that the Swedish Academy said created plays with a "blend of laughter and gravity that opens our eyes to abuses and injustices in society and also to the wider historical perspective in which they can be placed"? Because Fo was not widely known outside of Italy, the choice was highly controversial. But the award subsequently brought to world attention the unique work of this talented and provocative man who, in collaboration with his wife, Franca Rame, has created a substantial body of theatrical work. Fo and Rame have created more than seventy plays in the thirty-odd years they've been working together. And those years have been odd indeed.

Fo and Rame began their dramatic career together in the 1950s as a part of Italy's conventional theater circuit in Milan. But wishing to speak to a broader group of working people, they moved into the poorer neighborhoods and formed their own theatrical company. Using comic elements from the commedia dell'arte along with influences from Bertolt Brecht and seminal stand-up comic Lenny Bruce, the pair began creating plays that are both outrageous in their comedy and unsparing in their attacks on society's hypocrisies.

The plays are not merely entertainment; they are vehicles intended to expose corruption in the Italian government and the church. One of the most famous is *Morte Accidentale di un Anarchico* (*Accidental Death of an Anarchist*), which lampoons the police bureaucracy in the most outlandish ways. In the play, the mysterious death of an outspoken worker by police officers is based on a similar event that occurred in Milan in the late sixties. Here Il Matto, a maniac, impersonates a police officer at the station where the anarchist was killed. The maniac succeeds in exposing the real killers by making them literally and figuratively trip over themselves in a series of highly physical and comic scenes. "Nothing gets down deeply into the mind and intelligence as satire," Fo has said.

Another is *Non Si Paga! Non Si Paga!* (*We Won't Pay! We Won't Pay!*), which enjoyed an off-Broadway success in the United States in 1980. It begins with a strike over high supermarket prices by a group of irate housewives and continues with rebellions by commuters and factory workers until the entire city of Milan grinds to a halt. Once again, the seriousness of the situation—the rising cost of living—is underscored with broad physical comedy.

Together Fo and Rame have created a controversial body of work that continues to revitalize theater around the world. Whether they work together as cowriters, author and actor, or husband and wife, their union is a unique theatrical partnership. One of their collaborations, *Adulto Orgasmo Escapes From the Zoo,* is a series of monologues about women. Rame's feminist perspective combines with Fo's sense of the absurd to create unique portraits of women in society. In one of the monologues, "A Woman Alone," the protagonist is locked in the house by her husband and subjected to many forms of harassment, including obscene phone calls and sexual overtures, by a relative encased in a full-body cast.

Although the plays are written in Italian, they have been successfully translated into many languages and performed throughout the world. The universal themes of injustice, social hypocrisy, worker oppression, and male and female relations, combined with broad physical comedy and witty dialogue, speak to people everywhere. The work of Dario Fo and Franca Rame is a source of Italian pride because it courageously confronts difficult political issues and moves us to a greater awareness of social inequities.

57

Saint Francis of Assisi

The son of a wealthy merchant, the greatest and most famous Christian saint was born near the end of the twelfth century in the small village of Assisi in Umbria. He was christened Giovanni Bernardone but was early called Il Francesco (the little Frenchman) because his father traveled widely in France to do business.

As a young man, Francesco prepared for life as a soldier, engaging in the frequent wars that then erupted between the various Italian city-states. He was imprisoned for a year during the course of a battle between Assisi and Perugia. Shortly after his release he set out for Apulia to resume his military career but became ill on his journey and was forced to return home to Assisi. There he experienced a profound revelation that led him to abandon the military and devote his life to the service of humanity. He disposed of all his worldly possessions, giving them to the needy. A famous fresco by Giotto depicts Saint Francis giving his clothing to a soldier by the side of a road, and he is the subject of many great religious paintings portraying his humility and self-sacrifice. A lover of animals, he is oftentimes depicted communicating with a variety of God's creatures. Saint Francis dressed in rags and lived an ascetic life, gathering followers and traveling to Rome in 1209, where he obtained permission from Pope Innocent III to found the Franciscans, an order of Catholic brothers—not ordained priests—who would devote their lives to others and live in absolute poverty.

Two years before his death, the famous event occurred that was to assure his canonization. While praying on the Monte della Verna, near Assisi, he had a vision, and his palms began bleeding. This "miracle" was the first recorded occurrence of the stigmata, a phenomenon in which a devotee personally experiences wounds like those of Christ on the cross. This phenomenon was believed to have recurred regularly until his death in October 1226. As word of his death spread, Francis was mourned by his followers and devout Catholics throughout the world. In 1228, only two yeas after his death, Pope Gregory IX proclaimed him a saint. To this day, Italian Catholics celebrate October 4 as the Feast of Saint Francis of Assisi to commemorate the great piety and devotion of this holy, humble man.

58

Galileo Galilei

For centuries, under a system of astronomy invented by Ptolemy, the second-century Egyptian astronomer and geographer, the earth was thought to be the center of the known universe, with the sun, moon, and all other heavenly bodies revolving around it. This was the accepted view of the universe until the sixteenth-century Polish astronomer Nicolaus Copernicus, published a treatise on the revolution of heavenly bodies, which he dedicated to Pope Paul III. The pope, however, regarded such an idea as heretical because it diminished the role of humanity and made the idea of a special creation seem highly unlikely.

It just so happened that shortly after the publication of Copernicus's treatise, a brilliant Italian mathematician and astronomer at the University of Padua with two like-sounding names, Galileo Galilei, perfected a remarkable instrument, called a telescope, that allowed a close-up view of the heavens. This instrument, it was believed, could be put to use in the service of the church and quickly resolve the pernicious conflict between the church and the emerging science of the day. Galileo was summoned to Rome and ordered not to teach or disseminate the Copernican system but instead to use his telescope to demonstrate that it is the sun that moves around the earth and not the other way around. In 1632, Galileo upset his patrons by publishing a work that would not only confirm the discoveries of Copernicus but would also lay the foundation for modern scientific thought.

Galileo was arrested and brought to Rome for trial, where he was forced to retract his statements and accept the prevailing view that the earth does not move but is a stationary body at the center of the universe. As he rose from his knees after saying what his inquisitors demanded, Galileo mumbled a few words that have resonated through history: "*Eppur si muove,*" he said. "Nevertheless, it does move."

Galileo died blind and sick, under house arrest in Siena for his defiant insistence that truth arrived at through science is a more valuable and deeper truth than merely wishful thinking that supports preconceived ideas. In his final book, *Dialogues Concerning Two New Sciences,* published in the last years of his life (he died in 1642), Galilieo summarizes his remarkable contributions to the ways in which we understand the physical world today.

59

Marcella Hazan

"Classic" is the word that comes most readily to mind when thinking about Marcella Hazan, the reigning doyenne of Italian cooking in America. This is true not only because she is the author or coauthor of *The Classic Italian Cookbook, More Classic Italian Cooking,* and *The Classic Pasta Book* but because her attitudes and beliefs about Italian cooking are classic in nature, uncorrupted by politically or even nutritionally correct ideas about food and women's roles in preparing it. Her book *Marcella Cucina* is a marvelous and highly personal compendium of wonderful Italian dishes. How can you not love a woman who writes; "I am dismayed by the misguided attitude of those who champion olive oil over butter as though it were a cause. How do they make the sauces for their homemade pasta, I'd like to know, or the bases for most risottos?" Of course, the answer is they make them exclusively with olive oil, but for Marcella, making a risotto base without using a mixture of butter and olive oil is heresy.

Unlike so many trendy cookbook authors and culinary celebrities of the day, Marcella is not interested in "fusion of cross-cultural culinary hybrids"; she believes instead that cooking must reflect the place of its origins in both the distinctiveness of its ingredients and the style of its preparation. She also unashamedly (and very unfashionably) acknowledges the pleasure she has felt throughout her lifetime cooking for her husband. The recipes, she tells us, were created "for and because of" her husband, Victor, and the story of how she learned to cook as a young wife in a foreign city is well known to all Hazan enthusiasts. During these years, Marcella re-created the food she remembered from her childhood and preserved the heritage of Italian regional cooking.

But the miracle of Marcella Hazan's writing is not only that she regards cooking as an art but that she regards *eating* as one. "Eating in Italy," she writes in the introduction to *The Classic Italian Cookbook*, "is one more manifestation of the Italian's age-old gift of making art out of life." She shows us how Italian eating is related to the changing seasons and how it reflects the rhythms of nature. On a day when you're feeling a bit low, try one of Marcella's recipes, say, Fusilli with Creamy Zucchini and Basil Sauce or Cannellini Bean and Barley Soup and your day will begin to perk up immediately. Her recipes often take some time and patience, but that's because there are no shortcuts to creating "the real thing."

60

Italian Women

Let's take a moment to praise the achievements of Italian women. In a world dominated by male viewpoints, history often overlooks female contributions to history and culture. Here are some facts that history books often tend to gloss over.

At around the ninth century A.D. there lived a woman named Trotula of Salerno who was a prominent physician. In fact, the town of Salerno was known for its skilled female doctors. Trotula wrote a book, many centuries ahead of its time, called *The Diseases of Women*, which talked frankly about diet, exercise, and sex. She was a pioneer in modern women's health care.

During the Renaissance, with the advent of the printing press, many women took up reading and writing. Vittoria Colonna was a close friend of Michelangelo's and a poet in her own right. Isabella Andreini was one of the founders of the commedia dell'arte theater movement, writing and performing original plays and composing prose extolling the virtues of women. In the seventeenth century, Artemisia Gentileschi was a Baroque painter whose rape at an early age had a profound effect on her haunting works. Bloody, violent, and powerful, her paintings often depict the deeds of heroic women.

Today's Italy, unlike the United States, actually has an "equal rights amendment." What began with the Italian constitution in 1948 prohibiting sex discrimination has been amended to include maternal leave, professional training, and equal pay with 1977's Equal Opportunity Law and 1991's Positive Actions Law for Women. Women's business organizations have sprung up throughout the country, and their importance in the Italian economy continues to grow.

No field of endeavor is off-limits to the Italian woman of today. In the world of sports, there are hockey, basketball, soccer, and other leagues that are exclusively for women and have strong followings. Mountain-biking enthusiasts have a heroine in Paola Pezzo, who won the Olympic Gold Medal for Italy in 1996, the first recipient ever for the sport. The 1998 New York Marathon female first-place winner was Franca Fiacconi, who crossed the finish line at 2:25:17, the second-fastest time for a woman in the course's history.

Italian-American women have made history on this side of the globe and continue to push the boundaries of gender-biased roles. During World War II, when American men were overseas, thousands of women took over skilled machinery jobs that were important to the war's successful outcome. "Rosie the Riveter" became a national mascot, based on a hardworking Italian American named Rosie Bonavita.

Italian women continue to reshape and rethink their identities. Camille Paglia is currently on the cutting edge of intellectual history. Her book *Sexual Personae: Art and Decadence from Nefertiti to Emily Dickinson,* introduced her controversial opinions on gender roles, and her essays on art, culture, and philosophy continue to raise eyebrows. Paglia's "postfeminist" views include an unapologetic sexuality and a refusal to see women as "victims" of male oppression.

And the beginning of a new century promises more opportunity for Italian women to flex their muscles and expand their mental horizons. In America, the National Organization of Italian American Women (NOIAW) promotes pride through educational and social programs. In Italy, organizations such as FIDAPA (Italian Federation of Business and Professional Women) help women achieve career goals in the workforce and break free from traditional stereotypes.

61

Sophia Loren

In 1997, *Shape* magazine polled over four thousand women to determine whom they regarded as the ten "sexiest women in the world." Not surprisingly, current stars and models like Sharon Stone, Cindy Crawford, and Sandra Bullock figured high on the list, but only one of the women was not in her twenties, thirties, forties, or even fifties. Sophia Loren, a women in her sixties, continues to be regarded as one of the world's sexiest women.

For many, Loren is the epitome of Italian feminity. Her sculpted features, penetrating eyes, and charismatic presence have increased the popularity of dozens of Italian and American films. She is truly an international film star whose talent and devotion to her family have elicited the admiration of fans all over the world.

Loren was born Sofia Vilani Scicolone on September 20, 1934, in Rome and was raised in the seaport town of Pozzuoli at a time when war ravaged nearly all of Italy. So emaciated was she as a child that her friends called her Sofia Stuzzicandente (Sofia the Toothpick). But she blossomed as a teenager, and at age fourteen she won a beauty contest and shortly thereafter got her first role as an extra in the American film *Quo Vadis*, then being filmed in Rome. While competing in a second beauty contest, which she didn't win, she met her future husband, Carlo Ponti, the Italian producer who launched her career in the cinema.

That career has spanned a half century, including memorable performances in *The Pride and the Passion* (1957), *Desire Under the Elms* (1958), *Boccaccio '70* (1962), and *Marriage Italian-Style* (1964). Loren won an Academy Award for her performance in *Two Women* (1961) as well as a Lifetime Achievement Award from the American Academy of Motion Picture Arts and Sciences. With her incomparable screen presence, Sophia Loren is one of the truly elegant and beautiful women of our time.

62

Niccolò Machiavelli

Why should Italians be proud of a man whose very name has become an adjective representing ruthlessness, manipulation, and a lack of scruples? Because few writers have been misrepresented and misunderstood as much as Machiavelli has and because he remains one of the most influential and important political theorists of all time.

Nicolò Machiavelli was born in Florence on May 3, 1469, in the same year that Lorenzo de' Medici ("the Magnificent") assumed power and laid the groundwork for the reforms that were to convert the city-state into a self-governing republic. In the years 1494–1512, the Medicis were expelled from Florence, and in 1498, Machiavelli became a diplomat for the new Florentine government, often traveling abroad to represent its interests.

Machiavelli's political ideas can be found throughout his published works, which include *Discourses, The Art of War,* and the *History of Florence.* But he is most famous for the advice and analysis contained in his posthumously published manual of statecraft called *The Prince,* a book he wrote in 1513 (but was not published until 1532), after he had fallen out of favor when the Florentine republic was defeated by the Spanish army and the Medici family returned to power. Having been close to the center of power with the former government, Machiavelli was now regarded as a threat to the new state and was arrested, imprisoned, and tortured. After his release from prison, broken and humiliated, he returned to his family's farm in Sant' Andrea, south of Florence. There, during a period of recuperation, he wrote *The Prince,* dedicating it to Lorenzo de' Medici (the grandson of Lorenzo the Magnificent, whose enlightened leadership had transformed Florence) in hopes of regaining favor with the new government.

The Prince was conceived in the tradition of "advice books" of the time, generally written by intellectuals for royalty, usually informing them of the sort of gentlemanly behavior appropriate to their regal station. Machiavelli's book, however, went much further than earlier examples of the genre in laying out a philosophy of political leadership that has reverberated through the centuries.

Machiavelli believed that it is extremely difficult for a state to move from one form of government to another without swift, uncompromising, and resolute action. From this belief comes his reputation for encouraging ruthlessness. But that interpretation is incorrect, for it neglects his constant emphasis on the public good and the importance of what he called *virtù*—acting with moral integrity and honesty.

You can't always expect people to "do the right thing," and Machiavelli knew that. He has influenced political thinkers and politicians from Thomas Jefferson and James Madison to John F. Kennedy, Charles De Gaulle, and Margaret Thatcher. Because human nature remains constant, he will undoubtedly continue to be influential for years to come.

63

Madonna

Madonna is more than just a pop singer, an actress, and a celebrity. She is a phenomenon, one of the most talked about, photographed, loved, lusted after, hated, and worshipped women today. Madonna strikes a pose, and all the world watches. Since she exploded on the pop scene in the early 1980s, she has been constantly transforming both herself and pop culture.

Born on August 16, 1958, Madonna Louise Ciccone grew up in the suburbs near Detroit, Michigan. Her birth mother, also named Madonna, died when she was only five. As a young woman, Madonna moved to New York City, hoping, like thousands of other starstruck youths, to be discovered for her singing and dancing talents. Unlike most of the others, she was.

The phenomenon begins with the 1983 release of the album *Madonna*. With suggestively unkempt hair, stacks of bracelets, and "mix and match" thrift-store clothes, she writhed her way into the heart of the pop mainstream. She was no flash in the pan, either. Subsequent years brought additional albums, each showing a different side of this fascinating diva. With every release, she has sported a new look and a new sound. Her 1998 album *Ray of Light* is one of her most critically acclaimed and popular albums so far. Her fans have consistently supported her, and her detractors can't seem to get enough, either. Conventions, web sites, fanzines, and shrines swirl around her larger-than-life personality.

Why? She is a remarkable entertainer and, particularly, an excellent dancer. Her touring shows are vibrant and alive with rhythm and energy. And she is a wonderful singer, giving her melodies attitude and personality. She is an arbiter of fashion tastes; what she wears affects the look of the season.

In addition, she is an extremely smart businesswoman, in control of her life and career every step of the way. She owns her own record label, Maverick, which has had a string of successful releases.

And now she is a mother. Even in this role, she continues her life of controversy by daring to raise her daughter, Lourdes, as a single parent. Madonna's flamboyance and charisma go a long way toward shattering the stereotype of Italian women as submissive and subservient to men. This is a contemporary Italian-American woman who combines the passion of Italians with the practicality and business sense of Americans to forge a new identity that is uniquely hers.

64

Rocky Marciano

The Brockton Blockbuster, as he was known, had fists of steel. The Rock would land punches that buckled the knees of even the heartiest opponents. Forty-three of his forty-nine professional fights were won by knockouts. Born Rocco Francis Marchegiano on September 1, 1923, he was one tough cookie from the beginning. As an infant, he was already a heavyweight, weighing in at twelve pounds at birth and surviving a near-fatal case of pneumonia at eighteen months of age.

It wasn't until after he was drafted into the army that he discovered boxing. Stationed at Fort Lewis, he participated in amateur fights with great success. Upon returning home, Rocky decided to become a professional boxer. He began a regimented training schedule, running eight miles through the streets of his hometown, Brockton, Massachusetts, in weighted boots while tossing a football back and forth with his friend to ward off his mother's suspicions, who disapproved of the sport.

But Mama would soon be very proud of him. From his first professional fight on March 17, 1947, to his final bout against Archie Moore on September 21, 1955, Rocky was truly a champion. The man could not be stopped, slowed, or even hurt. During his career, he was only knocked down twice, spending a total of seven seconds on the canvas.

The U.S. Testing Company once measured the force of his punches, equating them with armor-piercing bullets and the energy necessary to spot-lift a thousand pounds a foot off the ground.

On September 23, 1952, in what is regarded as one of the greatest matches in the history of heavyweight boxing, Rocky stepped into the ring against then-current champion Jersey Joe Walcott. The fight was long, brutal, and exciting. By the twelfth round, though, Jersey Joe looked as if he had the title clinched on points. But the Rock was not finished. In the spectacular thirteenth round, Rocky landed one of his famous "Susie-Q" punches, sending Jersey Joe to the mat for the count. "Soon as it landed," Jersey Joe recalled later, "the lights went out."

Rocky successfully defended his title against all contenders, retiring undefeated at age thirty-two. In the ring, he was a powerful force to be reckoned with, but outside it, he was a true gentleman. His charm and spirit gave a dignity to the sometimes tawdry sport of boxing. Tragically, he died in a plane crash in 1969, but his legend lives on in gyms and boxing rings all over the world.

65

Michelangelo

To view his work is to visit a dimension of celestial ecstasy. His paintings, murals, and sculptures are doorways to a heightened state of being. They are the very essence of the word *masterpiece*. It's not only proud Italians who believe that Michelangelo Buonarroti was and is the greatest artist the world has ever known.

Michelangelo was one of the few Renaissance artists to come from a well-to-do family; his father was a city magistrate. Ludovico Buonarroti was none too pleased with his son's desired vocation and tried on numerous occasions to beat some sense into him. Fortunately, Lorenzo "the Magnificent" de' Medici stepped in and convinced the family that art was indeed among the noblest of all professions. As the result of living in the Medici household for a brief period, Michelangelo's artistic talents blossomed. Marsilio Ficino, Giovanne Pico della Mirandola, and Angelo Poliziano, some of the great intellects of the period, congregated there to think, drink, and perhaps sing a bawdy song or two.

It was Poliziano who suggested the mythological theme of one of Michelangelo's first great sculptures, *The Battle of the Centaurs,* a marble relief whose subject would become an important aspect of many of the artist's later works.

In the late 1400s, Michelangelo moved to Rome, where he carved *Bacchus,* another Roman-influenced sculpture, in 1496. His next piece, the poignant and moving *Pietà,* would represent the other passion in his art: Christian devotionalism. Here the classic image of a dead Christ lying across his mother's lap is conveyed with touching restraint but great emotion and energy. Michelangelo's feelings about this particular work of art must have been very positive, for it is his only creation that actually bears his signature.

Michelangelo returned to Florence in 1501 and began another masterpiece, the sculpture of *David.* In four years he turned a piece of marble into one of the most dynamic, captivating, and memorable sculptures ever created. This fourteen-foot statue shows a strong, determined David with his slingshot getting ready for his momentous battle with the giant Goliath. The fierce look on David's face was called *terribilità,* or "awesome power," and would forever be associated with Michelangelo and his work.

The way he breathed life into slabs of marble was simply divine. Michelangelo himself was often dumbfounded by his own powers. While chiseling *Moses* for Pope Julius II, it is rumored that he screamed,

"*Perché non parli?*" ("Why don't you talk?"), and threw the chisel at his creation, leaving a chip on *Moses*'s knee that visitors to the church of San Pietro in Vincoli in Rome, where the statue resides, can still see today.

Perhaps the greatest culmination of his art is the magnificent ceiling of the Sistine Chapel in Rome. Although he considered himself primarily a sculptor, this painted fresco is an unprecedented achievement. Working alone and lying on his back, he created a series of panels encapsulating the span of biblical history from the creation of man to the life of Noah. These paintings, rich in detail, provide a visual account of the Judeo-Christian view of world history that no one has equaled before or since. The image of God, reaching forth to give Adam, his creation, the touch of life is the very essence of terribilità.

In 1536, after the devastating sack of Rome, Michelangelo returned to the chapel to paint *The Last Judgment,* the largest fresco of the Renaissance, which also marked the era's end. The figures portrayed on the ceiling demonstrate a mastery of the human form that changed Western art forever.

Late in his life, Michelangelo began a friendship with the poet Vittoria Colonna, who inspired a great many sonnets and drawings. He died in Rome in 1564, leaving behind a treasury of artwork that established a standard for excellence in art that has never been surpassed.

66

Maria Montessori

"And so we discovered that education is not something which the teacher does, but that it is a natural process, which develops spontaneously in the human being," begins educator Maria Montessori in her book *The Absorbent Mind*. "It is not acquired by listening to words, but in virtue of experiences in which the child acts on his environment. The teacher's task is not to talk, but to prepare and arrange a series of motives for cultural activity in a special environment made for the child."

Those three sentences contain the essence of an educational revolution that has reverberated throughout the twentieth century, influencing the course of childhood education all over the world. Students of Maria Montessori have included Anna Freud, Jean Piaget, Alfred Adler, and Erik Erikson, a group of educators and child psychologists whose collective insights into how children learn are built on the foundation of Montessori's ideas.

Several aspects of those ideas are worth underscoring: First, Montessori saw learning as a *natural* process; we do not need to force children to learn—they are naturally curious and soak up new knowledge like sponges. Second, she believed that children learn by *doing,* not by being told how to do something. Third, she demonstrated how children flourish and learn in a stimulating environment, scaled to their own size and particular needs. These ideas are commonplace in classrooms throughout the country today, but when Montessori wrote her first book, *The Montessori Method,* in 1912, these ideas were still radical and very far from the prevailing practices in childhood education.

Maria Montessori was born in 1870 in Ancona, a port city on Italy's Adriatic coast. Although her intellectual interests were discouraged by her father and others around her who felt women belonged in the home, she remained steadfast in her pursuit of a scientific education. She made history when she graduated from the Medical School of the University of Rome, becoming the first woman physician in modern Italy. Her specialties, pediatrics and psychiatry, prepared her well for a career that would involve studying how children learn and putting her observations and insights into practice. Simple ideas like making classroom furniture an appropriate size for children and storing learning materials on low shelves where children could reach them revolutionized early education.

Today there are "official" Montessori schools throughout the world, and aspects of her method of educating children have infiltrated most public and private schools as well. Maria Montessori was clearly a woman whose ideas were well ahead of the prevailing wisdom of her time. She is unquestionably one of the most important educators of the century, and her revelations belong not only to Italy but also to the entire world.

67

Luciano Pavarotti

Italians take great pride in their outstanding tenors. Enrico Caruso, Mario Lanza, Ezio Pinza, and now Luciano Pavarotti have embodied that essence in the superb range of their highly trained and disciplined voices.

Luciano Pavarotti is clearly the greatest Italian tenor of his time and one of the few living classical artists who is a household name. He has toured the world bringing "the voice" with him—Pavarotti often refers to his voice as a separate entity—and thrilling audiences wherever he appears. His famous "Three Tenors" concerts and recordings with Placido Domingo and José Carreras have become one of the most successful and heralded ventures in classical music of all time.

Pavarotti was born in Modena, Italy, on October 12, 1935. His father was an amateur musician and instilled a love of opera in his son. Like his father, Luciano sang in the opera chorus of his local theater. His talent quickly stood out, and in 1961, when he was only twenty-three

years old, he won the Concorso Internazionale, a prestigious opera competition that offered as a prize a professional performance of a complete opera. Pavarotti made his debut as Rodolfo in Puccini's *La Bohème,* a role that was to figure prominently in his career.

In 1963, Pavarotti burst on the international opera scene when he substituted for an ailing Giuseppe di Stefano in performances of *La Bohème* with the Royal Opera at Covent Garden. The London audiences were amazed by the astonishing timbre of his voice and the sheer gusto of his performance. They heralded him as a "new Caruso."

Pavarotti's U.S. debut was with the great soprano Joan Sutherland in performances of Donizetti's *Lucia di Lammermoor.* Around the same time he premiered at La Scala in Milan, every opera singer's ultimate goal, again singing *La Bohème* with Mirella Freni under the direction of Herbert von Karajan. In 1968, the combination of *Bohème* and Freni worked its magic again for Pavarotti's New York Metropolitan Opera debut. His career blossomed in the seventies as he performed and recorded operas all over the world. Many of his performances became legendary, especially his rendition of Donizetti's *La Fille du Régiment*, which includes one of opera's most difficult arias. More recently, Pavarotti's repertory has expanded from lyric roles to heavier ones, such as Canio in Leoncavallo's *Pagliacci* and the title roles of Giordano's *Andrea Chénier* and Verdi's *Otello*.

Pavarotti today has passed beyond star status into the realm of cultural icon. He is known and recognized throughout the world as a man deeply committed to instilling a love of opera in future generations. One of his ongoing concerns has been the training of young singers, and he has even brought opera and his educational projects to Beijing, China, where he conducted master classes. His humanitarian efforts to aid the children of war-torn Bosnia have inspired musicians everywhere to participate in the various charity concerts he organized. His warmth, magnanimity, generosity, and great talent express what is very best about the Italian spirit.

68

Marco Polo

His recorded travels opened up an unexplored world for all to contemplate with awe and wonder. Traveling as a young man with his father, Niccoló, and his uncle Maffeo, Marco Polo journeyed to the distant lands of the East, where few Europeans had ever been before. There he discovered ancient China, its people and their customs, previously undocumented in the Western world.

The Polos were merchants who most of the time began and ended their journeys in Venice. Marco was born in 1254 while his father and uncle were on their first expedition to the East. Niccoló and Maffeo did not return to Venice until Marco was fifteen. During this long absence Niccoló's wife had died, leaving young Marco alone in the world. They quickly decided that Marco would accompany them on their trip back to the Mongol Empire to meet its illustrious leader, Kublai Khan.

In 1271 the Polos set sail with explicit greetings from Pope Gregory X to Kublai Khan, and this voyage can be seen as the beginning of

East-West diplomacy. In 1275 they arrived in what is now known as Beijing, and presented their letters to the distinguished Chinese leader. The great Khan and Marco took an immediate liking to each other, and for seventeen years Marco was his roaming ambassador, traveling throughout the Mongolian region.

After a twenty-four-year absence, in 1295 the Polo family returned to Venice for good, truly world-wise veterans. Marco continued to lead a life of adventure, joining the Venetian army and quickly becoming embroiled in the wars that plagued the Italian continent. In 1298 he was captured by the Genoans in the battle of Curzola and spent a year in prison.

While this time in prison was not the happiest period of Marco's life, it would be a boon for historians and dreamers of future generations. It was probably the first time Marco had actually sat still in his entire life! Within the prison walls, he dictated his travels, stories, and discoveries to his cellmate. The manuscript became known as *A Description of the World,* one of the most influential travel books ever written.

In it Marco describes the adventures of his young life in meticulous detail. He takes the reader along on his sojourns, describing Far Eastern cities and cultures that had never before been known to Westerners. He records local legends and thoroughly describes China's social stratification. Immediately upon its publication in 1298, the book was a sensation. Based on his writings, the then-unknown regions of the world were mapped and recorded.

There have always been those skeptical of the veracity of Marco's account of his travels. Some say he embellished many of his adventures and/or actually made up parts of them out of whole cloth. In the long run, however, whether the accounts are fact or fiction is unimportant. They are indisputably eye-opening, romantic, and inspiring. On his deathbed, at the ripe old age of seventy, he refuted his critics by saying, "I have not told half of what I saw." Fortunately, he did tell some, and his stories made the Eastern world a more familiar place for all Europeans.

69

Sacco and Vanzetti

Upon receiving the death sentence, the Italian immigrant Bartolomeo Vanzetti made a statement that has resonated for decades and has in fact been printed as poetry in anthologies of verse: "If it had not been for this, I might have live (*sic*) out my life, talking at street corners to scorning men, I might have die (*sic*), unmarked, unknown, a failure. Now we are not a failure. This is our career and our triumph. Never in our full life can we do such a work for tolerance, for justice, for men's understanding of man, as we now do by an accident. Our words—our lives—our pains—nothing! The taking of our lives—the lives of a good shoemaker and poor fish peddler—all! The last moment belongs to us—that agony is our triumph!" The statement is eloquent in its simplicity because it speaks for many immigrants and their heroic struggle for justice and fair treatment.

The case of Nicola Sacco and Bartolomeo Vanzetti ranks very high in the annals of injustices perpetrated by the American legal system in the twentieth century. Most historians agree that the evidence against them was scant, that the trial judge was severely prejudiced, and that the two Italian immigrants had reasonable and verifiable alibis for the crimes of which they were accused.

On April 15, 1920, at three in the afternoon, a brazen robbery occurred on the main street of South Braintree, Massachusetts, a small industrial town near Boston. A paymaster carrying a factory payroll and his guard were murdered by two gunmen, who fled with the cash boxes in a getaway car. Witnesses said the "gang" that perpetrated the crime numbered four or five and that they had swarthy complexions—like Italians. Having identified a vehicle they believed was the getaway car, the South Braintree police set a trap, luring Sacco and Vanzetti into it. Both were carrying guns at the time of their arrests—they were militant anarchists—and were eventually charged with the murders and robbery. Vanzetti was also charged with an earlier, similar attempted robbery in the nearby town of Bridgewater. In the summer of 1920, Vanzetti was tried and found guilty of the Bridgewater incident and was sentenced to ten to fifteen years in prison, an unusually harsh term for a first-offense attempted robbery. The verdict and sentence were portentous, however, and reflected the widespread prejudice against both Italians and political radicals that was rampant in America at the time.

The outcome of the Bridgewater trial convinced Vanzetti's lawyer,

Fred Moore, that the case was essentially political rather than criminal in nature, and he tried it accordingly. His defense strategy in the case was to assert that Sacco and Vanzetti were being accused not because there was hard evidence against them but because the state wanted to suppress the Italian anarchist movement, which encouraged individual freedom and sought to diminish government power. Moore's defense turned the trial into an international cause célèbre and enlisted the support of political activists throughout the world. Nevertheless, the jury found Sacco and Vanzetti guilty of both robbery and murder on July 14, 1921.

Moore's flamboyant handling of the case troubled some supporters of Sacco and Vanzetti because it took the focus off their essential innocence. He was replaced by a much more conservative lawyer, William Thompson, whose appeal of the verdict shifted the focus of the case to the legal issues involved. The fates of the defendants remained unresolved until April 9, 1927, when they were sentenced to die in the electric chair. The sentence was carried out on August 22 of that year and irrevocably became a symbolic gesture of the darker, intolerant side of the American character. The spirit of Sacco and Vanzetti is one of courage and determination, demonstrated by many Italian immigrants, to stand up for their rights despite the consequences.

70

Antonin Scalia

Justice Antonin Scalia is the first Italian American to serve on the U.S. Supreme Court. True to his heritage, he has brought a colorful passion to the normally stoic bench and has been a leader in reexamining ways in which contemporary courts have interpreted the Constitution.

Born in Trenton, New Jersey, in 1936 to Italian immigrants, "Nino," as he is known to friends, always had an interest in the law. He graduated first in his class at Georgetown University and studied law at Harvard. In 1982 he was appointed to the Federal Court of Appeals for the District of Columbia by President Reagan, and after only four years as an appellate judge, he was selected to sit on the Supreme Court.

Scalia's model of justice is based on concepts of "textualism" and "originalism," which he feels are essential to preserving the Constitution. "If the courts are free to write the Constitution anew they will, by God, write it the way the majority wants; the appointment and confirmation process will see to that. This, of course, is the end of the Bill of

Rights. . . ." he states in his book *A Matter of Interpretation: Federal Courts and the Law.* Scalia believes instead that justices must go back to the original text of the Constitution to determine what the founders had in mind when they drafted the document and use it as the framework for all decisions. Without that foundation, he feels, the country and its basic fundamentals, because they are open to the whims and fancies of any particular historical period, will collapse.

His deeply held beliefs have often made him the dissenting vote in near-unanimous decisions and a controversial figure on the bench. He feels, for example, that independent counsels tend to be politically motivated rather than neutral entities and has sought to curb their power. His methodology in forming his opinions has caused the entire Court to rethink how it interprets law, making it less susceptible to political influence. To be sure his own decisions are objective, Scalia has made it a practice of hiring a "counterclerk," someone whose opinions differ from his own, as a way of seeing all sides of an argument.

In the courtroom, Scalia's vivacious personality easily sets him apart from his fellow jurists. A quick wit and a fiery temper make him a lawyer's worst nightmare.

A father of nine, a devout Roman Catholic, and a lover of music and pasta, Scalia is an Italian American whose role on the Supreme Court truly impacts our lives.

71

Martin Scorsese

Martin Scorsese is a director's director and one of the most respected filmmakers working today. The range of his talent is enormous, and his knowledge of film and film history is legendary. When the American Film Institute put together a documentary history of American film, it chose him to narrate it and underscore his personal view of the American cinema. Scorsese was born in 1942 to an Italian-American family in Queens. His family soon moved to Manhattan, and he grew up on the streets of New York's Little Italy, which would be the backdrop for a number of his films.

He began his career in the sixties after attending NYU, where he made a number of acclaimed student films. His first feature-length film, *Who's That Knocking at My Door* (1968), impressed the independent filmmaker John Cassavetes, who became an important influence in Scorsese's life. Cassavetes encouraged him to "make a movie about something you really care about," and the result was *Mean Streets*

(1973), a film about Italians in New York that was a departure from what Scorsese calls the "*Mama Mia!* school of Italian acting." The film was widely acclaimed as a gritty portrait of New York street life and established Scorsese as an exciting, innovative director. It also made stars of actors Robert De Niro and Harvey Keitel, who gave impressive performances in the film.

Not wanting to be stereotyped as a director of Italian subjects, Scorsese next chose to do *Alice Doesn't Live Here Anymore* (1974), an odyssey of self-discovery from the viewpoint of a runaway housewife; it won an Academy Award for its star, actress Ellen Burstyn. Now widely regarded as a successful director, Scorsese undertook a series of films—*Taxi Driver* (1976); *New York, New York* (1977); *The Last Waltz* (1978); *Raging Bull* (1980); and *The King of Comedy* (1983)—that made it unmistakably clear his was a rare and inventive talent for the ages that was reshaping the look and style of American films. *Raging Bull,* the story of Italian-American middleweight boxing champion Jake LaMotta, was selected by critics all over the world as the best film of the 1980s and has become a classic of the American cinema.

But Scorsese did not rest on his laurels. He continued to make innovative and controversial films like *The Last Temptation of Christ* (1988), which depicts a very human Jesus, troubled by uncertainty and indecision, and *GoodFellas* (1990), which revisited the turf of *Mean Streets* and redefined the American gangster film. In 1993 he surprised nearly everyone by directing an adaptation of Edith Wharton's *Age of Innocence,* a nineteenth-century aristocratic romance. A project he has planned for the future is of particular interest to Italian Americans. Scorsese says that the film, called *The Neighborhood,* will examine three generations of an Italian family in America.

As a director of musicals, dramas, comedies, historical films, and documentaries (as well as an actor in several of his own films), Scorsese is the most honored American director of our time.

72

Frank Sinatra

For many people, the death of Frank Sinatra on May 14, 1998, marked the official end of the twentieth century—despite the fact that the calendar still showed a few more years remaining. In any case, an era certainly ended, for Francis Albert Sinatra was the quintessential entertainer of our time and one of the most imitated and influential male singers of *all* time. His career covered more than half a century during which he dominated several media. He recorded more than two thousand *different* songs and appeared in fifty-seven motion pictures; nearly all of his efforts in both media are stamped with his individual style and grace. His death led to an outpouring of tributes and surveys of his career that attempted to define that style, but at bottom it remains indefinable—distinctly his and ultimately not reproducible.

His voice, like another fine instrument crafted by an Italian—the Stradivarius violin—created a universally appealing and haunting musical presence. He invented a way of phrasing a popular song that made you feel as if he were singing directly to you, even when you listened to it on a record that you knew sold millions of copies. Although he sang a wide range of songs, his essential subject was a timeless one: love lost. Since nearly everyone has experienced that at one time or another in his or her life, Sinatra in a sense created a kind of collective musical shoulder for several generations of Americans to cry on. Though there are no statistics available, it's also a safe bet that more children were conceived with Frank Sinatra's music playing in the background than that of any other singer or musician. His most haunting music is for "the wee small hours of the morning," as one of his very best albums is entitled, though he was also capable of making us feel "Young at Heart" and taking it "Nice and Easy." He got under our skin and into our hearts and souls in a way that no other entertainer has, and for many it's simply hard to imagine a world without Frank Sinatra's music in it.

Former first lady Nancy Reagan, who was Sinatra's close personal friend, said that underneath the glamour and glitz, he was basically a conservative Italian-American man. In fact, you didn't need to dig deep to find that part of him. He was born in Hoboken, New Jersey, the son of an Italian-American fireman and a barmaid. The combination of tenderness and toughness that he embodied in his life, music, and films is an amalgam of the extremes of the Italian male character—tough guy and lover—to which Frank added an aura of vulnerability that was distinctly his. His Academy Award–winning performance as Angelo

Maggio in *From Here to Eternity,* a character *Newsweek* described as "a reckless, charming, hardheaded Italian-American with a streak of bullying pride," captures that essence.

We loved his voice, his charm, and his recklessness, and those who share his heritage are certainly very proud he was Italian.

73

Antonio Stradivari

In the city of Cremona, on the Po River in Lombardy, he made the finest musical instruments the world has ever known. Between the years 1666 and his death in 1737, he meticulously created by hand 1,116 instruments, including violins, violas, violincellos, and even harps, guitars, and mandolins. The estimated 650 of these that have survived are the most prized possessions in the musical world.

No violins before or since have ever produced the sheer clarity and purity of sound that his have, and each instrument that he crafted is a work of art unlike any other. So treasured are these masterpieces that the Library of Congress in Washington, D.C., has established a Stradivari Memorial, a temperature-controlled showcase of five Stradivarius violins and violas that are "consecrated in perpetuity to vital public service on the concert stage by distinguished artists." This memorial enables the greatest virtuosi in the world to perform on a "Strad" even if they cannot afford to own one, since they are valued in the hundreds of thousands of dollars. Albert Stern, a contemporary violin soloist who *is* fortunate enough to own one, waxes eloquent about the experience of playing his 1697 violin: "Valentino was said to have danced with women as if he were holding and playing a violin," Stern points out. "I play my Stradivarius violin as if I were holding a beautiful woman."

The secret of the incomparable Stradivarius sound remains a mystery; it has been attributed to the varnish the master used, the way the parts fit together, and the quality of the wood. In 1997, Dr. Joseph Nagyvary, a biochemist at Texas A&M University, said that the secret is in the soaking: Recent chemical analyses of wood from a Stradivarius violin show that the maple and pine that Stradivari used had probably been soaked in brine for a prolonged period of time. Nagyvary believes that this process can affect a violin's performance.

This rather unromantic explanation may interest chemists, but whatever the reason for the sound, a Stradivarius makes music like no other instrument. It weeps and sighs, turning the highest notes into an ethereal longing and the deeper range into a profound desolation. In the hands of a master, this blend of wood and strings produces a hauntingly divine sound. It's little wonder that the imprint of Antonio Stradivaris of Cremona adorns what has become the most cherished violin label in the world.

74

Giuseppe Verdi

His music has become synonymous with Italian pride. The more than two dozen operas that constitute his musical career are heartfelt dramas that resound with a sense of patriotism that was sweeping the country during the Risorgimento, that period in the early-to-mid-1800s when a nationalistic sentiment was growing stronger, eventually culminating in the unification of Italy in the latter part of the century. You could say that Verdi's operas became the soundtrack for this movement. Passionate, provocative, and filled with unforgettable melodies, many of his works struck a chord in those Italians who were engaged in a struggle to create a national identity.

Verdi was born in 1813 in Le Roncole, a small town near Parma, to a family with no history of musical talent. But something in the young genius inspired him to learn music and become an organist at the local church. When he applied to the prestigious Milan Conservatory, however, he was rejected. Still, Verdi was not discouraged, and he began to study with Vincenzo Lavigna, a composer and former musician at La Scala in Milan.

His first two operas, *Oberto* and *Un Giorno di Regno* (A One-Day Reign), were not successful. Then tragedy struck. Verdi's wife and two children succumbed to illness and died. Deeply traumatized, Verdi vowed never to compose again, but a libretto was forced upon him by a director at La Scala. It was from this profound grief that his music reached another level.

The resulting work, *Nabucco,* was unequivocally Verdi's first masterpiece. The opera told the story of Jewish exiles whose persecution in their own country was something with which the Italians could identify. The opera's lyric *"Va pensiero, sull'ali dorate"* ("Our thoughts go out on golden wings") became an unofficial Italian anthem during the period and still carries emotion today.

Verdi's output continued strong, with *Rigoletto, Il Trovatore,* and his most famous opera, *La Traviata* (The Wayward Woman). This later opera is a tragic tale of the life and love of a young woman, Violetta, outcast by the bourgeois society in which she lives. Its pure melodies and heightened drama have made it a favorite of performers and theatergoers alike for more than a hundred years.

During this productive period, Verdi averaged over an opera a year. As the call for unification grew louder, a popular exclamation was "Viva VERDI," a tribute to the composer but also an acronym for *V*ittorio *E*manuele, *Re D'I*talia, who would become the country's first king. In 1861, as tribute to his music and passion, he was given the title "Honorary Deputy" in Italy's first Parliament.

He continued to write music until the 1890s, completing two of his finest operas, *Otello* (1887) and *Falstaff* (1893), late in life. Based on Shakespearean characters, these works add yet another dimension to Verdi's great musical achievement. He died in 1901, a national hero and a world-renowned musical artist. The harmonious strains of his powerful operas live on in productions everywhere.

75

Leonardo da Vinci

There are countless words that can be used to describe Leonardo da Vinci: painter, sculptor, astronomer, botanist, zoologist, geographer, mathematician, physicist, architect, musician—the man had a fertile mind. Many believe he was the greatest intellect of all time.

Born in 1452 in Vinci, between Pisa and Florence, Leonardo da Vinci was the illegitimate son of a Florentine notary and a peasant woman. He studied art under Andrea del Verrocchio, whose workshop was a training ground for some of the most important artists of the Renaissance. It quickly became clear that Leonardo's talents reached far beyond those of his peers. *Annunciation* and *Adoration of the Magi* (incomplete) testify to his early genius. Around 1482, he left Florence for Milan to work for Lodovico Sforza, under whose patronage he flourished. *The Virgin of the Rocks* and the *Last Supper,* two surviving works from his first Milanese period, are evidence of his amazing mastery of form and color.

But Leonardo had only begun to tap into his many talents. When plagues ravaged Milan in 1484, he turned part of his attention to city-planning projects. His mind continued to expand from there, and he recorded most of his highly advanced thoughts in a series of notebooks, describing and drawing preliminary designs for then-unimaginable objects and concepts like flying machines and tank warfare. Scattered throughout his copious notes on painting itself were revolutionary notions about line and perspective that heralded the Renaissance era's shift of focus from the divine to the human.

These notebooks are Leonardo's greatest legacy. When he died in 1519, he left them to Francesco Melzi, who kept them hidden until his own death in 1570. Additional notebooks, long believed lost, were discovered at the National Library of Spain as recently as 1965 and were published in 1974 as *The Madrid Codices.* Taken together, Leonardo's notebooks reveal a man whose gift for innovation was unparalleled. His mind sought out the impossible and tackled ways to achieve it. His drawings and inventions, showing the potential for human achievement, were the catalyst for thousands of projects. He created science fiction and left it to future generations to make it science fact.

It's not surprising that Leonardo left numerous works unfinished, since just one of his ideas would represent a lifetime of work for anyone else. (Imagine how he must have struggled to harness them all!) When he sat down to create his art, it was only natural that he applied his scientific side as well, using perspective and drawing the human form in a realistic manner. His paintings, finished or unfinished, contain so much life and character that they are considered masterpieces (see chapter 15).

A thinker, a dreamer, a doer, and a visionary, Leonardo da Vinci is the original Renaissance man. His work is a testament to the infinite possibilities of the human spirit. It is difficult to think of anyone who has inspired more Italian pride.

76

Harry Warren

You might not realize it, but the tunes you sing in the shower may be it of a great Italian-American composer! In fact, you wouldn't realize it even if you knew the composer's name, because Harry Warren couldn't sound less Italian. In fact, Warren wrote the music to some of the most popular American standards ever.

He was born Salvatore Guaragna in Brooklyn in 1893, but the Guaragna family, like many Italian immigrants during this period, opted to change their name to an "American" one because of the rampant prejudice they experienced.

"I remember as a child I had no interest in being Italian, only in being an American," he said. "Strangely, many years later, as an adult, I got to appreciate my Italian background and thought about sometimes going to Italy to live."

From 1932 to 1957, Harry Warren, paired with a variety of lyricists, including Johnny Mercer, Mack Gordon, and Al Dubin, produced over 250 songs for motion-picture musicals, which were then in their golden age. From this output, an astonishing fifty titles are considered standards and are sung and played almost daily somewhere in the world. One of his earliest successes was his music for the film *42nd Street* (1932), with two big hits in "Shuffle Off to Buffalo" and "You're Getting to Be a Habit With Me." From there, it was only up, up, up.

With *Gold Diggers of 1933* (1933), the melodic mind of Warren gave us "We're in the Money," a song whose hopeful lyric and catchy tune helped ease the pain of the Great Depression. With its sequel, *Gold Diggers of 1935* (1935), Warren earned an Oscar and gave us "Lullaby of Broadway," another unforgettable song in his growing catalog of hits.

And they just kept coming. "Jeepers Creepers," "You Must Have Been a Beautiful Baby," and "I Only Have Eyes for You" are further examples of songs that are so successful that they are remembered apart from the films for which they were originally written. While some people only know a line or two of the lyrics, Warren's melodies are ingrained in their minds.

Warren and his partners wrote for all of the major Hollywood studios and worked with some of their brightest stars. Fred Astaire and Ginger Rogers sang and danced to his music, as did Judy Garland, Betty Grable, and Doris Day. Even Carmen Miranda shook her fruit basket to the beat of Warren's meter.

His pairing with "Big Band" leader Glenn Miller produced landmarks in both of their careers, with "Chattanooga Choo Choo" and "Serenade in Blue" becoming bona-fide classics.

And we, as proud Italians, can especially enjoy "That's Amore," a song from the Jerry Lewis–Dean Martin film *The Caddy* (1953). Martin's playful vocal rendition made it *the* love song of the fifties; it introduced Americans to a whole range of Italianized expressions, like "signore," "pasta fazool," "vita bella," and "scusa mi." The song was reintroduced and repopularized when it was used as part of the soundtrack to the hit film *Moonstruck* (1987).

So why doesn't anybody know who Harry Warren is? Because he preferred to stay out of the limelight, letting his music speak for itself. Always the wit, Warren quipped: "Even my best friends don't know who I am."

Warren died in 1981. Only a few remembered his name, but he gave the world songs that will be sung and remembered for a long time.

PART IV

FOOD

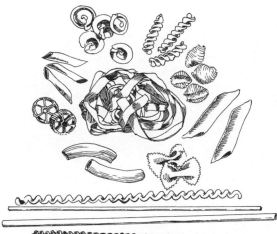

77

Antipasti

Antipasto literally means "before the meal," and it is a custom in Italian homes never to keep people waiting for food. As soon as guests arrive, they are served an antipasto a piedo, an appetizer that they can nibble on even before they are seated. There is usually another, more substantial antipasto served *a tavola* (at the table) that precedes the first course of dinner. Some antipasti are very elaborate and require nearly as much effort to prepare as a main course, but most are quite simple and can be put together very quickly. What could be simpler, for example, than slicing and peeling a cold, ripe cantaloupe in eights and wrapping each slice with a razor-thin slice of prosciutto? The mixture of the ripe, fruity texture and sweetness of the melon with the salty fleshiness of the prosciutto awakens the palate and prepares it for the wide range of flavors of whatever meal follows.

Some people like to make a whole meal of antipasti, and why not? Next time you're at a good Italian restaurant, think about bypassing the entrée altogether and ordering a sampling of these wonderfully distinctive Italian appetizers. You might follow the prosciutto and melon, for example, with some roasted asparagus or some clams with tomatoes and capers; perhaps some grilled calamari might be just right after that or some mozzarella with parsley and garlic; add a bean and salami salad with some breadsticks, some Sicilian olives marinated in olive oil and rosemary, or all of the above. The delightful thing about antipasti is the variety of tastes they provide and the sense of abundance and diversity they bring to the table.

Antipasti are either cooked or raw but in either case are almost always served with crusty bread or breadsticks. A particularly elegant "raw" antipasto is carpaccio, very thinly sliced, chilled raw meat or fish (of a particularly premium grade) lightly sprinkled with olive oil, various herbs, and shaved parmigiano cheese. The dish is said to have originated at the famous Harry's Bar in Venice in 1950 when the owner, Giuseppe Cipriani, prepared it for a patron whose doctor had forbidden her to eat cooked meat. Originally made with paper-thin slices of first-grade beef and served only in gourmet circles, carpaccio today is also made with veal, tuna, and salmon and can be ordered in many Italian restaurants.

Antipasti are the perfect way to begin any meal.

78

Balsamic Vinegar

Balsamic vinegar is a secret Italians kept to themselves until the mid-1970s, when Chuck Williams of the Williams-Sonoma cookware and gourmet-food chain in the United States discovered it and imported some for sale in his stores and catalogs. This occurred at the same time that the fashion for lighter, more flavorful food dishes, called nouvelle cuisine in French and nuova cucina in Italian, began sweeping the culinary world. Creative chefs discovered in balsamic vinegar just the right combination of pungency and sweetness to give the new dishes an exciting and unorthodox flavor. In the last few decades it has become a staple of gourmet cooking in the United States and throughout the world.

Although cheap imitations of balsamic vinegar are now produced in many countries, the real thing can only be found in two small provinces in northern Italy: Modena and Reggio. The reason for this is that making this kind of *aceto* (vinegar) is labor-intensive and requires a knowledge of special processes that have been passed on from generation to generation in this region since the fifteenth century. Unlike other kinds of vinegar, it is not made from wine but from the "musts" (i.e., the skin and pulp) of crushed grapes that are heated, aged, and stored for very long periods. First-rate balsamic vinegar is at least twelve years old, and extra vecchio types can be aged for up to a century! Naturally this latter type is very rare and costly. Italians classify it as vinegar *da bere* (for drinking) instead of merely being used *da condire* (as a condiment or dressing). The culinary scholar Burton Anderson reports that Lucrezia Borgia "used Modena's vinegar as a tonic for body and soul."

By the 1990s the imitation rip-offs calling themselves "Balsamic Vinegar of Modena" had become so widespread that the Italian government passed legislation banning the use of the term *balsamico* and any reference to either Modena or Reggio for anything other than the traditional vinegar produced in the region. Of course, Italian laws can be enforced only in Italy, which has not stopped producers in other countries from continuing to turn out inferior products that are misleadingly labeled. But in Modena, the Consorteria di Aceto Balsamico Naturale, described as "an association of twelve hundred producers, master tasters, and devotees," keeps the faith by holding a competition each June in the town of Spilamberto, near Modena. There the producers of the region, who take great pride in their product, vie for the coveted Palio di San Giovanni Prize, awarded annually to the vinegar that the judges deem best from the twelve hundred or so entries submitted.

True balsamic vinegar has a syrupy, nearly caramel texture that offers the palette the delight of opposing tastes simultaneously. It fills the mouth with an explosion of flavor that lingers happily as a mild and pleasant aftertaste. Just a few drops of it can turn a drab salad into a culinary adventure.

79

Basil and Tomato

Is there a marriage of herb and vegetable (well, technically herb and *fruit*) more clearly made in heaven than the combination of basil and tomato? Try this experiment: Take a (preferably homegrown) vine-ripened tomato and cut it into quarter-inch slices from top to bottom. Spread the slices—overlapping one another in a circle—on a plate. Insert a single basil leaf between each slice. Sprinkle very lightly with salt and freshly ground pepper. Drizzle a little extra virgin olive oil over the slices and sit down in a sunny place with a knife and fork to savor your creation. Eat slowly, one small bite at a time, making sure you always have a bit of basil as well as tomato on the end of your fork. After you do this, you'll probably replace the expression "Stop and smell the roses" with "Sit down and savor the basil and tomatoes."

The tomato, introduced throughout Europe sometime in the sixteenth century, was believed to have aphrodisiac properties; when you taste the lush gorgeousness of a fresh tomato on a sunny day, you will understand why. The Italian name for tomato—*pomodoro* (golden apple)—probably derives from the color of one of its varieties, but it may also have to do with the high value that the Italians accord this incomparable fruit.

Today the tomato appears everywhere in Italian cooking, particularly in the south. And where the tomato goes, can basil be far behind? Virtually every sauce that includes tomatoes calls for basil to give the sweet, juicy flavor of the tomatoes a fuller, livelier taste—to "kick it up a notch," as television chef Emeril Legasse is fond of saying as he adds outrageously spicy ingredients to one dish or another. But basil does not overpower tomatoes as some herbs and spices do to the foods they flavor. Instead, it deepens and ennobles the tomato's essential flavor, reminding us that both plants are gifts of the earth's bounty. The ancients regarded *basilico* as a sacred plant, to be cut only with specially designed instruments, made of pure metals, after proper rituals had been performed. Legend has it that Saint Helena discovered the "True Cross" under a basil patch, further sanctifying the herb for Christians.

No Italian garden is complete without enough tomato plants and fresh basil to perform the celestial marriage again and again. Their union is a distillation of the essential flavors of Italy—sweet, earthy, pungent, and lingering.

80

Cheeses

Although cheese in America has been vilified in recent years because of its generally high fat content, in Italy cheese remains a central element in diet. Italian cheeses are known the world over for their distinctive taste, heady aroma, and unusual and diverse texture. Cheese of various kinds complement other foods and add depth and complexity to ordinary flavors. What's a dish of pasta without a generous sprinkling of parmigiano cheese atop it? And think of what a delight a slice of tomato can be when paired with a slice of mozzarella di bufala.

In fact, those two cheeses, parmigiano and mozzarella di bufala, are prime examples of the cheesemaker's art, and although they are widely imitated all over the world, there are simply no substitutes for the real things, made with care and craft in Italy. The kind of parmigiano that comes pregrated in a cardboard tube and is widely sold in supermarkets has the same resemblance to authentic Parmigiano-Reggiano, made in the Emilia-Romagna region of Italy, that rhinestones have to diamonds. In addition, it is one of the healthiest cheeses around, having the lowest cholesterol content of any of the world's major cheeses. Mozzarella di bufala, made from the milk of water buffalo, is such a fresh, moist, delicate cheese that it needs to be preserved in water; unlike ordinary mozzarella, it suffers when you melt it.

There is gorgonzola, a pungent, rich Italian version of blue cheese that makes a marvelous accompaniment to grapes or walnuts and a spectacular pasta sauce. There is provolone, a cheese packaged in long tubes and tied with ropes that one can see hanging from the ceilings of Italian delis; it is excellent sliced with cold cuts on "hero sandwiches." There is ricotta—a soft, creamy cheese that is as much at home with fruits and salads and desserts, such as cannoli, as it is with rich pasta dishes, such as ravioli, manicotti, or lasagna. And there is the marvelous and delectable marscapone, a dessert cheese that is the main ingredient of that omnipresent Italian dessert tirami sú.

This listing is the mere tip of the iceberg of Italian cheeses. Some others are tallegio, asiago, romano, pecorino, fontina, and scamorza. When Charles de Gaulle said of France: "How can you govern a country with 246 varieties of cheese?" he might well have been speaking of Italy, whose varieties exceed that number. Come to think of it, that may be one of the reasons Italy changes governments so often!

81

Dolci (Sweets)

Italians generally do not eat a great many sweets. There are, of course, some marvelous Italian desserts, but they do not accompany daily meals; they are instead reserved for special occasions—Sundays and holidays—when there is a celebrative mood in the air and when uncles, aunts, and cousins join the family table. At such times, someone in the family is dispatched to the local pastry shop and comes home with a boxful of assorted Italian pastries that are as delectable to the eye as they are to the tongue.

The king and queen of Italian pastries are cannoli and sfogliatelle. Of Sicilian origin, cannoli are tubes of crisp, fried pastry dough filled with ricotta cheese and a wide variety of other ingredients, including, but not limited to, chocolate chips, dried fruits, or nuts. Cannoli are very rich and filling, and aficionados of this confection will travel for miles to a pastry shop to find them. Not quite as rich, sfogliatelle are triangularly shaped pastries made of thin, layered flakes of pastry dough wrapped around a moist, creamy filling. They often have an almond flavor, although it's difficult to compare them with anything else, since their taste is absolutely special.

Cannoli and sfogliatelle can be found today throughout Italy and in nearly all Italian-American communities. Other Italian pastries and desserts vary from region to region. In addition, they are often prepared seasonally, like the panforte, or strong bread of Siena, a dense fruitcake that adorns Sienese Christmas tables. Zeppole di San Giuseppe is a fried, sweetened puff of pastry dough made especially for the feast of St. Joseph's Day throughout southern Italy, though it probably originated in Naples. Cassata is a rich, spongy Easter cake made in Sicily. The panettone of Milan is made both at Christmas and at Easter, and large baking companies, like Motta or Perugina, package these elaborately and distribute them to Italian groceries and delis everywhere.

Also available throughout the world now are dozens of varieties of biscotti, long, dry cookies that are excellent for dipping into wine or coffee. Biscotti are often baked with almonds or other nuts and sometimes coated with chocolate (although purists will resist this innovation).

Since Italians invented *la dolce vita* (the sweet life), it's not surprising that their desserts are so delectable.

82

Espresso

Remember when a cup of coffee was just that and not a highly specialized beverage that can appear in dozens of different forms? For the many varieties of coffee popularized in the United States by Starbucks and other coffee bars that now dot the American landscape coast to coast, we can thank Italians, who have taken pride in making distinctive coffee drinks since the early 1700s. The variety of those drinks accelerated in the early twentieth century when the *macchina a vapore,* the elaborate steam espresso machine that you now find all over the world, was invented in Naples.

Perhaps because Italy grows no coffee of its own, Italians quickly found the drink both exotic and stimulating and established it as the bracing way to put a night's sleep behind them and move on into the activity of the new day. Italians patronize their favorite espresso bars each morning on the way to work for their quick fix. For the most part, they like their coffee much stronger than Americans do, and caffè

Americano is the name of a watered-down espresso served in a large cup rather than the egg-sized demitasse cup that is used for espresso alone. The word *espresso* refers to the manner in which the coffee is made: Steaming hot water is pressed through a small amount of finely ground, tightly packed coffee beans, expressing a concentrated, nearly syrupy stream of liquid. True aficionados like their coffee *ristretto* (tight), meaning they only want the coffee expressed from a single pull of the steam lever. This fills about a third of a tiny espresso cup and is swallowed in one gulp like a shot of whiskey. Less hardy souls take regular or *doppio* (double) espresso, or even caffé lungo, a full cup of espresso that has been considerably weakened. At the other extreme, there are those who like their caffé corretto, coffee "corrected" with a shot of grappa or brandy.

Add milk to the coffee equation and you have a whole other category of drinks beginning with cappuccino, espresso with steamed milk, topped with the creamy foam from the steamer. Caffé latte is similar to cappuccino but leaves off the foam topping, and latte macchiato is primarily warm milk "marked" or "stained" with a bit of coffee. Children are often served coffee this way to prepare them for a serious coffee-drinking career as adults. In all, Italians drink over 9 *billion* cups of coffee annually, which is a lot of java no matter how you brew it. It's no wonder they're all so animated!

83

Garlic

A famous Italian restaurant in San Francisco's North Beach called the Stinking Rose serves garlic in virtually all its dishes. Their slogan is "We season our garlic with food." You can order a garlicky pesto, a tomato sauce with garlic, chicken with garlic and herbs, lamb with garlic puree, shrimp sautéed in garlic and oil, pasta of all varieties served with garlic, and even an appetizer of just plain roasted garlic that has the texture of a mashed potato and is much more subtly flavored than you might imagine. And, believe it or not, you can top your meal off with a delicious serving of (try to imagine this) garlic ice cream!

The menu of the Stinking Rose may sound extreme, but garlic aficionados tend toward extremes, and for them a meal without *allium sativum* (the scientific name for garlic) is something like a day without sunshine. You'll get through it, but it just doesn't quite satisfy. The use of garlic in foods is ancient, and the herb has been prescribed medicinally since at least 1500 B.C., when it was listed in an Egyptian document as a remedy for over twenty ailments, including headaches, insect bites, tumors, and heart problems. The herb supposedly had magical properties as well. In Homer's *Odyssey,* Odysseus uses a garlic bulb to prevent Circe from transforming him into a swine.

While Italians can't claim to have originated the use of garlic as a primary culinary herb, they certainly have taken to it with gusto and enthusiasm. An Italian household at dinnertime without the smell of garlic in their air is rare, and the various pairings of garlic and oil in Italian cuisine create a signature flavor for distinctive dishes. One of the simplest and most authentic Italian dishes is spaghettini aglio e olio c peperoncino rosso, comfort food for many Italians at almost any time of the year. Here is a version you can enjoy at home:

Start boiling water to make a pound of spaghetti. While you're waiting, peel and mince 6 cloves of garlic, then peel and thinly slice another 6 cloves. Heat 1/2 cup olive oil over medium-low flame and add the sliced garlic; stir gently for about 15 seconds, until lightly browned. Remove from heat. Meanwhile, after the spaghetti is finished cooking, drain it, return it to the pot, and add 1 can of chicken broth. Then add all the garlic, along with 6 tablespoons of chopped parsley and as much parmigiano cheese as you like. Sprinkle red pepper flakes on individual portions, to taste. *Buon' appetito!*

84

Gelato

Other countries may have ice cream, but Italy has gelato, a thick, sticky, creamy concoction that is custard-based and unlike ice cream made anywhere else. The very best gelato is made in small batches by individual ice cream vendors in their own shops. You can find them in nearly all Italian cities, with the sign *Produzione Propia* (Made by the Proprietor) hanging in the window.

The father of Italian gelato is Francesco Procopio dei Coltelli, a Sicilian aristocrat who established a chain of coffeehouses throughout Europe in the late seventeenth century. In 1675 he opened the Cafe Procope in Paris, where he sold Viennese-style ices and developed a new kind of frozen dessert that was much richer than the ices because it was made with eggs and cream. The new gelato was a great success, and Procopio began producing it in his coffeehouses throughout Italy and the rest of Europe. His rivals, seeing a good thing, followed suit, and the *gelateria* (ice cream parlor) was born.

A particularly familiar version of gelato originating in Naples is spumone (usually misspelled in the United States as "spumoni"), a molded wedge of three flavors of ice cream—vanilla, strawberry, and pistachio—whose white, red, and green colors mirror the colors of the Italian flag. (Italians seem to be particularly fond of foods that are imbued with patriotic fervor. Red, white, and green risotto, made with tomatoes, cream sauce, and pesto, as well as pizza Margherita, made with tomatoes, mozzarella, and basil, are other examples of this trend.)

Another popular kind of Italian ice cream preparation often featured in Italian restaurants in the United States is tortoni, made with frozen vanilla mousse, macaroons, almonds, and rum, usually served in a paper cup. It originated in the Parisian confectionery stores owned by the Italian Tortoni family.

While gelato is more and more available in large cities in the United States, a true upscale Italian gelateria is a wonder to behold. Tubs of delicious flavors greet the eye behind polished glass. Chrome fountain fittings gleam; waiters and waitresses are stylishly clad. Enter one of these establishments on a warm summer night, order a coppa con panna (a dish of gelato with whipped cream), and you are transported to a world of pure indulgence, tempered by order and style—a definition of most things Italian.

85

Italian Meals

Italian meals are not just served; they are orchestrated. The major meal in Italy is served in the middle of the day. (Virtually everything is closed except restaurants between one and four in the afternoon, when the entire nation pauses to eat.) In Rome, many people go home for dinner and then return to work, giving the city four rush hours!

An Italian meal will not be hurried. It begins with an antipasto or, when guests are present, several antipasti. There is an antipasto a piedi, which literally means a "standing" appetizer served immediately upon the guests' arrival before they are seated at the table. This is often some type of bruschetta: toasted slices of Italian bread served with various toppings, such as chopped tomatoes, pesto, olives, cheese, and garlic. Then there is an antipasto a tavola, an appetizer for the table—perhaps salami, cheeses, stuffed pepper or artichokes, or any of dozens of other savory choices, all served with a fresh, crispy Italian bread, or focaccia. The antipasti are followed by a *primo piatto* (first plate), which is nearly always either soup or pasta, or perhaps a soup with pasta, like tortellini in brodo (stuffed pasta in broth). The *primo* is naturally followed by a *secondo*—a main entree, usually meat or fish prepared according to regional tastes. (In fact, there is no such thing as generic Italian food; all Italian cooking is regional. You're more likely to get seafood in Apulia, meat in Bologna, with the possibility of either or both in Naples and Rome.) A *contorno* (side dish), which consists of a vegetable like zucchini, asparagus, broccoli rabe, or green beans, accompanies the secondo. A good regional wine, such as Chianti or Sangiovese, is poured generously alongside all of this to "wash it down," as the Italians say.

After a fish or meat dish, Italians like to cleanse their palette with a fresh salad, or insalata, served either as a side dish or at the end of a meal. But the meal is not quite over—a plate of fresh fruit and cheese makes an appropriate final touch. Italians rarely eat dessert with daily meals, but on Sundays or holidays a tirami sú or cannoli makes a delectable finale, accompanied by a cup of very strong espresso.

The sheer splendor of an Italian meal is a marvel to behold. We can take pride in our spirit of *abbondanza* (an abundant table), which no one ever leaves hungry.

86

Lasagna

You're having a bunch of friends over for a casual dinner, and you want to make something that's delicious, filling, and doesn't cost a fortune. What better choice than lasagna, that Italian staple that seems to always appear in some guise or another at potlucks, group meals, buffets, or wherever there are many mouths to feed. Lasagna can be traced back to the ancient Romans, who definitely knew something about feeding large numbers of people. They prepared flat strips of baked dough called *laganum* that could be cut up in pieces and passed around along with the meat, fish, grapes, and wine that crowded the tables at a Roman feast. The word itself, however, more likely derives from the Latin *lasnia*, which refers to a cooking pot.

Lasagne are wide, flat, thin sheets of pasta that are briefly boiled, then layered in a baking dish and interspersed with whatever the chef feels like putting there on any given day. An early recipe for lasagna dates from the fourteenth century and reads (in English translation) as follows: "Take good white flour and knead it with lukewarm water to make your dough. Then roll it out thin and let it dry. Cook in chicken consommé, or consommé from other fat meats; then put it in a platter with grated *cacio* cheese, layer after layer, as many as you please. Bake." Although the modern cook is more likely to purchase dried lasagna and add sauce, mozzarella, and other ingredients to the layers, the basic concept remains the same.

The variations of lasagna are endless, and it has become one of the most Americanized Italian dishes. (To be sure, it has also been Mexicanized, Frenchified, and Britishized.) The most authentic Italian versions, however, are those of Bologna and Naples. In Bologna, where the Bolognese claim modern lasagna originated, it is often made with spinach noodles and layered with several kinds of meat and balsamella, a thick, white sauce made with milk, flour, and butter. The Neapolitan version is layered with tomato sauce, ricotta, and mozzarella.

But when making lasagna, there's no need to be orthodox. The ingredients you put in it are limited only by your imagination. It's a wonderful dish for vegetarians, who can layer it with zucchini, mushrooms, tomatoes, broccoli florets, and all sorts of herbs and spices. Melted cheeses give it additional heft and texture. Or, if you're not feeling too imaginative, buy a box of your favorite noodles and follow the recipe on the package. Whatever crowd you happen to be feeding will undoubtedly be thankful.

87

Olive Oil

Ask an Italian chef what item in the kitchen cupboard he or she could absolutely not do without and nine out of ten times the answer will be olive oil. Olive oil imparts its distinctive flavor to Italian cooking. It's used in pasta sauces, as part of the famous Italian salad dressing of oil and vinegar, as a base to coat and sauté vegetables in, as part of a marinade for meat or fish, or even as a dip on its own for crusty Italian bread. From a nutritional point of view, one of the best things about it is that it is monounsaturated oil and does not affect the level of cholesterol in the blood. This is surely one of the reasons why the heart-attack rate in Italy is considerably lower than in the United States and why Italian food is essentially good for you as well as delicious.

Olive oil comes in a variety of different styles and grades, and the seasoned cook knows which one to use for each dish. Extra virgin olive oil is the premium grade and does not mean, as some joker once said, that the olives have never even *thought* of sex. What it does mean is that the oil with this designation has been made from the first cold pressing of the fruit.

In order to understand the importance of this process to the quality of the oil, you need to know a little bit about how olive oil is produced. The best oil is produced from olives harvested by hand or collected from shaken trees by nylon nets. It is essential that the olives not touch the ground, because when caked with soil, they quickly become rancid and acidic. After harvesting, the olives are stored for several days so that some of the water they contain evaporates, allowing the oil to become purer and more intense. Then the olives are crushed under huge granite stones, and the resulting pulp is layered on mats of nylon or, for purists, straw. The mats are stacked four or five high, then pressed in a hydraulic press. The oil that results from this first cold pressing is called *extra vergine.* The pulp is then heated and spun in a centrifugal cylinder to produce additional, but necessarily inferior, oil.

As you can gather from this brief description of the process, producing fine-quality olive oil is as much an art as producing fine wine from crushed grapes. Great olive oil is just not made in large quantities, and it's understandable that the mass-produced, exported oil you find on supermarket shelves is vastly inferior to what you can buy at a small grocery in a Tuscan village. It may be a little selfish, but the Italians keep the very best for themselves. They're proud of the long heritage of producing great oils that are recognized as being of the finest quality.

88

Pane (Italian Bread)

While Italians would certainly agree that humanity cannot live by bread alone, they would also argue that it cannot live without it. Fresh bread daily is a necessity throughout Italy, and each region's bakers work through the night to create the fresh, crisp loaves of all shapes and sizes that are the very stuff of life in the country. An Italian meal served without bread is unthinkable; it accompanies every course, and in some cases it *is* the main course—as with bruschetta (thin slices of toasted bread brushed with olive oil and herbs) or pancotto (cooked bread), a peasant dish of bread turned into a stew with tomatoes, garlic, and olive oil. One can substitute rice or soup for pasta, vegetables or fish for meat, and do without dessert altogether, but there is no substitute for the bread that graces an Italian table. And when the pasta or main course is done, the bread is used like *un pezzo di lana* (a piece of wool) to soak up the sauce on the plate.

Bread in the south tends to be large, round loaves, often made at home. It is densely textured, usually torn apart by hand rather than sliced and passed around the table with great gusto and animation. In Apulia, the heel of Italy's boot, where the large, round loaf thrives, consumption of flour products, primarily bread and pasta, makes up a substantial part of the day's diet. According to food historian Waverly Root, the average Apulian consumes between 1.75 and 2.2 pounds of flour *per day!*

In the north the bread is lighter, longer, and crispier. Here the loaves are often long and thin, excellent for making "hero," or "submarine," sandwiches. Slice one horizontally, top with tomato sauce and mozzarella, heat in the oven, and you have an instant pizza.

In both the north and the south, the bread varies from village to village and from city to city. Nowhere but in Milan can you find the round, semihollow rolls called michetti that the Milanese love to butter and enjoy with their morning espresso or cappuccino. Only in Ferrara can you get ciupeta, a round loaf with four points adorning it like a crown. It is made from a wheat grown in the area that produces a distinctive semolina flour called *soglia.* In Padua they sing the praises of their pan padovan (Paduan bread), which they believe is the best in Italy.

And so it goes, the bread of each region distinguishing itself in the same way as the wine. "A loaf of bread . . . a jug of wine . . . and thou," the poet said, and Italians know exactly what he meant.

89

Pasta

There is surely no more versatile, better-loved food on the planet than pasta and no food more quintessentially Italian. Although many culinary scholars have dispelled the notion that Marco Polo introduced pasta to Italy when he returned from the Orient with noodles, that myth persists. Wherever it originated, its Italian varieties are endless. The names of pasta are usually related to its shape: farfalle means butterflies, and the pasta is shaped like one, penne are shaped like quills or pens, even spaghetti comes from *spago* (string).

Many of the same-shaped pasta have different names in different regions. What is called fettucine in Rome is called tagliatelle in Bologna. What is fusilli in most of Italy is incannulate in Apulia, and so on. Each region has its distinctive pasta preparations as well: orecchiette (little ears) with greens is a specialty of Apulia; tagliatelle with meat sauce, or ragú, is the signature dish of Bologna; ravioli originates in Genoa, and pappardelle, a wide egg noodle usually served with a veal or lamb sauce, is characteristic of Tuscany.

The secret of the triumph of pasta as an ubiquitous dish all over the world is its simplicity and adaptability. Take a little flour, add a little water or eggs, knead it a bit, roll it out, cut it up in whatever shapes you wish, and there you have it: pasta fresca (fresh pasta) ready to be made al dente (chewy to the tooth) in boiling water and served with any one of hundreds of sauces with which you choose to flavor it. Of course, if you don't have time for all this, there is the even more ubiquitous pastasciutta, dried pasta, which you can take right out of the Ronzoni or DeCecco box, boil in salted water for a few minutes, and serve, again with whatever flavorful sauce you choose.

As pasta has become an international food, many variations on these Italian basics have emerged. A dish of penne with sun-dried tomatoes, chicken-breast strips, and shitake mushrooms, which you can find in many upscale California restaurants, is only remotely related to its Italian origins. On the other end of the food spectrum, a Kraft macaroni-and-cheese snack may seem even less Italian, but both speak to the remarkable flexibility and adaptability of this wonderful food the Italians have given the world.

90

Pasta Sauces

Pasta by itself comes in a delightful variety of sizes and shapes, but it requires embellishment and adornment if it is to be turned into a memorable or classic Italian dish. Throughout the Italian peninsula are the diverse sauces that become signature dishes of various regions, families, or chefs. Some of these achieve international renown, like the famous fettuccine Alfredo, which originated in Alfredo's restaurant in Rome and spread throughout the world after it became a favorite of Hollywood movie stars Mary Pickford and Douglas Fairbanks.

Tomatoes are the basis of one kind of pasta sauce, but even here variety is the key concept. There are sauces made with fresh tomatoes, cut, sliced, crushed, or puréed and blended with numerous additions. There are also sauces made with canned tomatoes of all types as well as with tomato paste that is squeezed from a tube. A classic marinara (mariner's style) sauce, made with fresh tomatoes and herbs, is so called because it was made by fishermen's wives who awaited their husbands' return with the catch of the day, which was added to the already-prepared sauce.

There are dozens, if not hundreds, of varieties of pasta primavera (spring pasta), but all of them are made with fresh vegetables and served throughout the spring and summer. Then there are various meat sauces, or ragùs, which run the gamut from sauces made with sliced chicken or ground beef to the extraordinarily baroque ragù de-nobili of Emilia-Romagna, which includes pancetta (Italian bacon), sausage, chicken, chicken giblets, pork, and beef!

Sauces made with shellfish (mussels, clams, lobster, shrimp) and other creatures of the sea (octopus and squid are Italian delicacies) as well as sauces made with all kinds of mushrooms *(funghi)* add to the vast spectrum of pasta additions, as do nuts, cheeses, breadcrumbs, eggs, cream, butter, and virtually every other edible item you might find in your refrigerator or cupboard.

Some sauces are really not even "sauces" in the traditional sense; rather, they are additions to the pasta that enliven and enrich it.

A good Italian chef knows that fresh ingredients combined with a little ingenuity can make a sauce sublime. It's a lot more than just tomatoes and garlic.

91

Pizza

"When the moon hits your eye like a big pizza pie, that's amore." Dean Martin sang the well-known Harry Warren tune, forever associating pizza with love. In the same song he tells us that that connection is particularly true in "Old Napoli," where pizza is a soul food, treated with a reverence akin to a religious experience. In Naples there is even an Associazione Vera Pizza Napoletana (Association for Authentic Neapolitan Pizza) that certifies restaurants making Neapolitan pizza with a sign they can display in their windows like the Good Housekeeping Seal of Approval.

The secret of great pizza—and what Italians take pride in—is its simplicity and the use of fresh ingredients. Pizza originated as a "street food," and to this day it remains one of the few Italian foods people often eat "on the go" rather than as a sit-down meal. There are pizza shops throughout Italy—especially in Naples and Rome—that display a wide variety of rectangular pizzas sold by the slice to businessmen and women as well as tourists on the move. One of its most celebrated varieties, pizza Margherita, is named for Italy's Queen Margherita, who visited Naples in 1889 and was charmed by a particular tricolore pizza made especially for her with basil, tomatoes, and mozzarella, ingredients whose green, red, and white colors represented the colors of the newly adopted Italian flag. (Italy did not become a single nation until 1870.)

Whatever ingredients adorn it, pizza is not pizza unless the crust is memorable. The thickness of the crust differs from region to region in Italy (as well as in America). What Americans call Chicago-style pizza, made in a deep dish and with a thick, bready crust, is essentially Sicilian pizza. Authentic Pizza Napoletana has a paper-thin crust that is crisp and well done on the bottom and soft and slightly undercooked on top, where the dough has been covered by the ingredients. Getting the crust to the right consistency is an art form and is very difficult to achieve in a home oven where maximum temperatures are not high enough to bake the dough quickly and evenly. Wood-fired ovens, which have always been used in Italy and have now become popular in the States, reach temperatures of 750 degrees Fahrenheit and are essential if you want the real thing.

92

Polenta

There is probably no more basic food in the entire Italian menu than polenta. Slowly add a cup of cornmeal to a quart of rapidly boiling water, stirring frequently for about an hour, and you have polenta, which is essentially cornmeal mush. The texture of polenta differs depending on how long you cook it and how long you wait before serving it. When served immediately, it is hot and creamy; if it is allowed to sit for a while, it becomes thick and solid and can be served in slices.

Polenta is found mostly in the northern provinces and is a staple in the Lombardy region of Italy, where it is often served in place of pasta or risotto. But it can be found in the south as well, where it is prepared with distinctive variations. And like those two other mainstays of the Italian kitchen, what makes polenta interesting is what is added to it rather than the cornmeal itself. In Apulia, where they love shellfish, you can get polenta al sugo di mitili, a polenta with a mussel sauce poured over it; in Piacenza, a town in the Emilia-Romagna province, they make a specialty called polenta e ciccioli, which is made by adding onions and pork crackling to the cornmeal toward the end of its cooking. Venetians love a dish with the charming name of polenta e oselèti scapài (polenta and the little birds that got away), although the only conceivable bird aspect of the dish is the chicken livers that accompany the bacon, mushrooms, veal, and sage that are the main ingredients. In the Piedmont area you will find plenty of polenta grassa, a layered dish of polenta and fontina cheese baked in the oven until it is browned on top. An alternate version of this is the polenta pasticciata, or polenta pie, of Lombardy, where layers of cold polenta alternate with layers of butter and grated cheese and are then baked.

Perhaps the most famous polenta dish of all is polenta coi osei, polenta with tiny songbirds that are spit-roasted, their juices mixed in with the cornmeal. This dish might appropriately be called "polenta and the little birds that didn't get away." It's a bit exotic (and even troubling) for American tastes, but they love it in Bergamo and Venice. The ingenuity of Italians in enlivening this simple peasant dish knows no limits. Polenta is comfort food Italiana, and it will add heartiness and warmth to any meal.

93

Restaurants

Until the mid-1970s, many Italian restaurants in America could be described in pretty much the same way: They were mostly neighborhood mom-and-pop operations, usually started by immigrant families hoping to bring some of the food and culture of Italy with them into the New World. Since most of the immigrants came from the south, southern Italian food predominated, particularly Neapolitan fare, with its heavy emphasis on thick, heavy tomato sauces.

Both the decor and the menus of these restaurants were remarkably similar: Often the booths and tables were covered with red-checkered tablecloths; straw-clad Chianti bottles served as candleholders and sometimes hung from the ceiling. The menu offered a few kinds of pasta, and sometimes lasagna and ravioli. There were also various pizzas and sausage-and-meatball sandwiches. Until about 1975, this type of menu is what came to mind when most Americans thought about Italian food.

Then something happened that changed all that. A new generation of entrepreneurs began creating restaurants throughout America that drew on a much wider variety of Italian cuisine, and trendy, upscale, mostly northern Italian eateries began springing up in major cities throughout the country. The decor of these restaurants reflected the style and fashion we have come to associate with contemporary Italian designers and the menus included lighter and more diverse dishes, influenced by new Italian chefs. Dishes like veal picata, salads of arugula or radicchio and goat cheese, fetuccine with seafood or mushroom sauce were introduced to the American palate. These restaurants also brought with them the Italian appreciation for fine wine and offered extensive, carefully thought out wine lists to their patrons. Some of them evolved into regional or national chains, like Il Fornaio, bringing with them a whole new level of culinary sophistication.

Today both kinds of restaurants thrive and complement one another. The local pizzeria down the block or around the corner offers a down-home heartiness and comfort that the more fashionable restaurants simply can't compete with, while the stylish Tuscan dining room offers exciting meals for very special occasions that are well beyond the capabilities of the average mama and papa. Americans have come to understand that Italian food is a reflection of the passion and culture of the Italian people and is just as diverse. It's not just spaghetti and meatballs anymore.

94

Risotto

The word for rice in Italian is *riso,* and it comes in many varieties. Risotto is neither a word meaning rice nor a particular variety of rice; rather, it refers to a particular way of preparing it. Risotto is to the city of Milan what pasta is to the rest of Italy. Unlike most rice dishes in which water or broth and rice are simmered together until the rice absorbs all the water, risotto is prepared by adding broth a little at a time and stirring constantly as the broth is gradually absorbed. This process produces a rich, creamy texture unlike any other rice preparation. Risotto is usually made with arborio rice, a short, stubby grain that "plumps" when you cook it.

Risotto Milanese is seasoned with the world's most expensive spice—saffron—and that lends the dish not only a remarkable flavor but a unique yellow color that is as distinctive as it is aesthetically pleasing. Like pasta, there are many ways to flavor and season risotto—with mushrooms, seafood, various meats, parmigiano cheese, vegetables, and herbs and spices.

To make a first-rate risotto to which you can add nearly any ingredient, you'll need a cup of arborio rice, 22–30 ounces of heated chicken broth, 1/2 cup of white wine, and an onion, peeled and chopped. In a large skillet, sauté the onion over medium heat in a mixture of olive oil and butter—and 1 tablespoon of each. When the onion is translucent, add the rice and stir with a wooden spoon until it is coated and begins to brown very slightly. The remainder of the process separates cooks from impatient eaters who don't like to stand over a stove. Risotto needs tending, like an infant. Gradually add about 1/2 cup of chicken broth, stirring continually for a few minutes until absorbed. Continue adding broth in this way—1/2 cup at a time—until all the broth is gone. Then add the wine, stirring until absorbed. When the rice is plump and creamy, add whatever you desire—chopped parsley, sautéed mushrooms, cooked shrimp, chopped vegetables, or some combination of all of these.

This is a dish you can serve with pride either as a main course, as a primo piatto, or as a side dish with chicken, meat, or seafood. And when there's some left over, you can make risotto al salto (jumping risotto) by mixing it with scrambled eggs and flattening it into a pancake. Now *that's* Italian.

95

Seafood

Since the Italian boot is a peninsula surrounded on three sides by water, it was inevitable that seafood would be used substantially in the Italian diet. Frutti di mare (shellfish, literally "fruit of the sea"), especially mussels, clams, shrimp, and lobster, as well as other types of fish (cod, flounder, whitefish, swordfish, and dozens of other local varieties) abound in Italian cooking in nearly every region, particularly in the coastal areas. The Adriatic Sea is less salty than the Mediterranean and as such is a primary source of Italian seafood. In cities along the Adriatic coast, like Venice, Ravenna, Rimini, Ancona, Pescara, Bari, and Brindisi, there is almost always a local *pescheria*, a fresh fish market where the *pescatore* (fishermen) distribute their daily catches.

One of the world's most famous seafood dishes originated in Italy but was modified on San Francisco's Fisherman's Wharf, where the Italian immigrant fishermen created a version of a soup from Genoa called burrida, or ciuppin, using fish harvested along the Pacific Coast. The result was called cioppino, and it is as hearty a concoction of seafood stew as you're likely to find anywhere. Cioppino can include a wide variety of fish. Genovese burrida typically is made with eel, palombo (a sort of mackerel), dogfish, and octopus, while the San Francisco version often includes salmon, shark, and clams. Both dishes are heavily seasoned with oregano, onion, bay leaf, and white wine, and usually mixed with tomatoes and potatoes. Though it is now served in restaurants in all parts of the country, aficionados insist that only in San Francisco can you get the real thing.

Octopus and squid, while not for the squeamish, are eaten in nearly all parts of Italy and are a particular treat in Apulia, where the rite of preparing octopus for the market is a spectacle to behold. Fisherman pummel octopuses against the pavement with a wooden paddle until they become tender and flower shaped. They are then displayed symmetrically in wicker baskets, where they are sold to customers eager to take them home.

Fish in Italy is sometimes marinated, but more often merely seasoned with a variety of herbs, including oregano, dill, parsley, rosemary, sage, and basil. It is often served whole and sometimes baked in a crust of salt (this method seals in the natural flavor of the fish) or broiled on a very hot grill. Italian seafood is both healthy and delicious. What more can we ask of it?

96

Stuffed Pasta

Pasta is one thing, but pasta ripiena (stuffed pasta) is quite another, and it is best prepared, as Fred Plotkin, a well-known authority on Italian food, tells us, by a virtuous cook who is "loving, patient, attentive, practical, decisive and, when necessary, speedy." These virtues are needed for the care and precision required to prepare the many varieties of filled pasta that include, but are certainly not limited to, ravioli, tortellini, agnolotti, cappeletti, manicotti, and other pastas, which have in common only the fact that they are made of pasta dough wrapped around some other ingredients.

Each of these varieties has its own history and rationale for being, and often the stories associated with them are the stuff of legend. Perhaps the most famous of these explains the shape of tortellini as resulting from the hopeless love of a Bolognese cook for his master's wife. Driven to distraction by the sight of her nude, he headed straight for the kitchen, where he fashioned a pasta ripiena in the shape of her navel! An alternate version of the origins of tortellini tells us that it was modeled not after the navel of a Bolognese aristocrat but that of Venus, the goddess of love.

The origins of ravioli are less romantic. The word probably comes from a word in the Genovese dialect, *rabiole* (things of little value). They were called this because they were often made of meats, vegetables, and cheese left over from previous meals. The table scraps could be mixed together, then wrapped in pasta dough and served again to make an entirely different meal. Ravioli were particularly popular with Genoese sailors because they could bring variety and substance to shipboard meals. It is believed that Columbus's sailors ate dried, cheese-filled ravioli on their voyages to the New World.

Today ravioli and other stuffed pastas have a much more festive association than their origins would suggest. Because they require a significant amount of time to prepare, they are usually served only on holidays or special occasions at home, although you can eat them any day of the week at most Italian restaurants. Sometimes the fillings for the pasta are associated with particular holidays; for example, the remarkable Christmas ravioli of the Abruzzi region of Italy, which is filled with a mixture of chestnuts, chocolate, almonds, citron bits, honey, cinnamon, sugar, and rum. In Emilia-Romagna, ravioli is stuffed with marmalade or marzipan for the feast of Saint Joseph. More common stuffings for ravioli are chopped meats, cheeses, fish, or vegetables.

Of course, today you can buy ravioli, manicotti, tortellini, and many other kinds of stuffed pasta ready-made in the freezer section of your local supermarket. It's not quite as much fun as shaping it from the navel of a loved one, but it will still turn a meal into a very special occasion.

97

Tirami sú

Imagine a dessert so scrumptious and irresistible that it has its own website devoted to singing its praises and directing devotees to restaurants throughout the world where they can find it. Such is the case with tirami sú, the ultimate Italian dessert made with angel food cake (ladyfingers), mascarpone cheese, liqueur, and varieties of espresso or chocolate. This is a "melt in your mouth" kind of dessert, with flavors and undertones that transport your tastebuds to a utopia to which they long to return again and again.

Tirami sú literally means pick-me-up, and legend has it that this refers to reviving sexual prowess. More likely, however, it simply refers to ending a weighty and substantial Italian meal on an up note—something special to help you pick yourself up from the table.

The essential component of tirami sú is mascarpone cheese, a sweet, distinctive triple-crème cheese made from the milk of cows fed on a special diet. It is produced in Lombardy and Emilia-Romagna and can now be purchased in quality supermarkets throughout the world. Mascarpone is a fresh and creamy cheese, textured somewhere between butter and whipped cream. It can be used in a wide variety of dishes, but in tirami sú it becomes a heavenly cloud of sweet sensations.

Tirami sú is actually a contemporary revision of a traditional Italian dessert called zuppa inglese (English soup), named because English artists living in Florence were particularly fond of it. Zuppa inglese contains ingredients similar to tirami sú, substituting custard for the *mascarpone. The Dictionary of Italian Food and Drink* credits the El Toulà restaurant in Treviso with originating the dessert in the 1960s. It took a while for its fame to spread, but in the 1980s it became a popular menu item in San Francisco's North Beach Italian restaurants and has now become a staple at Italian restaurants everywhere.

What does tirami sú taste like? Let me quote from Craig Miyamoto, who describes himself as a "self-styled, self-proclaimed, semi-professional tirami sú gourmet" on the aforementioned "tiramisu" web site he created and maintains: "Imagine that you're dressed in gossamer. You have delicate white wings and are sitting on a fluffy cloud. You are experiencing the greatest dessert ecstasy of your life. You are in Heaven, and Heaven is in your mouth."

98

Vegetables, Italian Style

The most valued resource in an Italian kitchen is not *in* the kitchen at all but is often very close to it: the garden. *"Dalla terra alla tavola"* ("From the earth to the table") is a phrase that captures the Italian insistence that the produce used to prepare daily meals is freshly harvested.

An Italian vegetable garden is characterized by variety as well as abundance. An absolute basic is several varieties of tomatoes, with plantings staggered throughout the spring so that the crop will come in continuously throughout the summer and early fall. Additional staples include zucchini, red and green peppers, broccoli rabe, eggplant, carrots, celery, peas, and as many kinds of lettuce as can fit in a planting area. Onions, scallions, and garlic are produced in their own separate spaces, and essential herbs include basil, oregano, rosemary, Italian parsley, tarragon, and thyme. If there is room, the garden will also include several kinds of beans, cauliflower, asparagus, fennel, and spinach. A garden of this type produces a succession of vegetables that allows a cook to avoid the blasphemy of canned or frozen produce. An exception to this is tomatoes, which form such a central part of the Italian diet that they need to be available all year round. For this reason, canned tomatoes or, preferably frozen tomato sauce made from the summer harvest are perfectly acceptable.

Meals are shaped by what seems ready to eat *today*. A cook wanders into his or her garden "listening" to the vegetables, observing the exact moment of redness when a tomato is ready to be picked, the exact size and tenderness that will make a remarkable zucchini dish or just the right hue of green or red to pluck a pepper from its stalk.

Because vegetables are grown with such care, it is important that they be cooked in a way that preserves their mature flavor. As with pasta, Italians always cook vegetables al dente—a texture that your teeth can bite into. This is achieved by steaming the vegetables briefly or sautéing them lightly in olive oil. Vegetables are served as a meal in themselves, as a side dish, and sometimes as an addition to pasta or risotto.

Once you get used to eating fresh vegetables the Italian way, the mere thought of canned spinach, frozen peas, or overcooked string beans makes you lose your appetite.

99

White Truffles

Called "the Mozart of mushrooms" by the composer Rossini, white truffles are one of the most expensive foods on the planet. Though the fungus is found throughout Italy, much of the world's supply comes from the little river towns of Alba and Asti, both about thirty-five miles from Turin, in Italy's Piedmont province.

Part of the mystique of white truffles comes from the manner in which they are harvested. In the dead of night, *trifolau,* or truffle hunters, roam the hills of Piedmont during the damp, foggy nights of late fall with dogs specially trained to sniff out the distinctive aroma of these "white diamonds" that are buried in the earth. They are then dug up, brushed off, and loosely wrapped in cloth napkins. Each night's harvest is brought to town, where vendors gather in secret to trade their wares. Although the Italian government attempts to control the truffle trade through licensing and value-added taxes, this is literally an underground business with its own secret codes and rituals.

The truffles dug up from the earth around Alba and its vicinity make their way through various middlemen to the gourmet shops of the world and then to the most elegant tables. There they are very thinly sliced and tossed with warm, buttered noodles (just one of many preparations) to create a dish whose exquisite aromas and flavors defy description. The trouble is that a white truffle smells and tastes like nothing else; thus, flavors to compare it with do not easily come to mind. We can talk about wines having lingering cherry, pear, or oak flavors and the like, but a white truffle tastes like . . . well, a truffle. The adjective most often used to describe it is "celestial," because there is nothing else on earth like it. There are, of course, black truffles as well, but these are much more common and have none of the mystical qualities associated with the tartufi bianchi. Excellent-quality white truffles are so rare and in such great demand that the Italians export very few of them. Like their olive oil, they keep the best for themselves. So if you really want a taste of this exquisite and rare mushroom, you'll need to make an autumn pilgrimage—as many do—to one of the many restaurants in Alba or Asti that create extraordinary dishes with this local treasure. You may have to mortgage your house to pay for it, but it will certainly be one of your most memorable meals ever!

100

Wine

Italians love their wine. To eat dinner in an Italian home and not partake of the wine is insulting to the host and does damage to the meal itself because Italian wines so eloquently complement the country's food.

While Italian wine-grape growers produce grapes for both red and white wines (as well as "blush" or rosé wines), it is the red that contains the soul of Italy and that generates the romance of Italian wine. If a table for two in a candlelit restaurant with a bottle of fine Chianti Classico and a carpaccio (thinly sliced, seasoned raw beef) appetizer is not enough to kindle a romance, then you'd better look for another partner.

In the northwest provinces, dark, thick-skinned Nebbiolo grapes produce the deep, rich Barolo and the lighter, more elegant Barbaresco wines from the many vineyards near the town of Alba. This area also produces the popular Barbera and Dolcetto wines in great abundance. The Valpolicella, Bardolino, and Soave wines you find in so many

American supermarkets are generally produced in the northeastern sector of the country, where producers like Bolla and Masi export them in great quantities. From the center of the country, in the region around Tuscany, comes Italy's most characteristic wines, Chianti and Chianti Classico, which are what most Americans think of when they think of Italian wine. The same area also produces the prestigious "Super Tuscans" from the Cabernet and Sangiovese grapes. The best of these Tuscan wines are coveted by collectors throughout the world and are often auctioned off at mind-boggling prices. The wines of the south are generally less well known in America and are not considered as prestigious as their northern rivals, but they are just as magnificent a complement to any meal.

A wide range of wine-making skills can also affect the quality of a vintage. In 1966 the Italian government established a system for controlling the quality of wine production and assuring consumers that certain wines met standards of taste, aroma, longevity, alcohol content, color, acidity, and so forth. If these standards are met, the wine maker is entitled to print DOC (for *Denominazione di Origine Controllata*— Denomination of Controlled Origin) on the wine label. Truly outstanding vintages are labeled DOCG, the "g" standing for *garantita* (guaranteed). While these designations are often highly subjective, they do provide some guidance to the nonexpert wine buyer shopping for Italian wines.

Italian wine is the very blood of the earth drawn upward through the vine into nature's own storage containers; clusters of grapes, bursting with juice and flavor, are then squeezed from the grape and stored in barrels to age and ripen. When bottled, it becomes a time capsule for the year and place it was made. Open a bottle of 1990 Montepulciano d'Abruzzo, for example, and you're transported to the very earth of the Abruzzi in south-central Italy, where the grapes are grown.

Recently, scientific studies have shown that wine, when consumed in moderation, is actually good for your heart—a secret many Italians seem to have known for a long time.

And the Final Reason . . .

101

Mama

While the father in Italian families is most often its head, the mother is unquestionably its heart and soul. Italians venerate "Mama," who is the source of a family's nurturing, its emotional center, its spiritual and moral guide. The role of the Italian mother is usually traditional, though, like all women, she has been affected by the winds of change that have shattered gender stereotypes and altered the roles of women in our time. In second- and third-generation Italian-American families, it is not uncommon for women to work outside the home. Nevertheless, in many Italian homes, the mother remains in charge of the domestic sphere, while the father is the primary breadwinner. To some this may seem old-fashioned and even reactionary, but for many Italians there is no more noble work than raising a family, and Mama's absolute devotion to one of life's most central tasks is a source of great pride.

An Italian mother is often a cook and counselor, interior decorator, fashion consultant, seamstress, nurse, accountant, and just plain friend in need. She dispenses food and advice accompanied by great portions of love. Like the conductor of an orchestra, she manages the music of family life through good times and bad and tries to maintain its emotional balance. Italians, it is well known, are emotionally intense, and Italian family life can often be, to an outsider, a cacophony of noise and commotion. Mama keeps the family functioning through all of its sound and fury.

It is said that the Italian devotion to the Virgin Mary emanates from the adoration of the mother. Italian men, the story goes, find it embarrassing to worship a male God but have no trouble devoting themselves to the mother of God, since they are so deeply attached to their own mothers. While Italy is not exactly a matriarchy, "Mama" is a powerful and central figure in Italian life. And she usually makes terrific marinara sauce as well!